Twice-Born World

Stories of Lithuania

Wendell Mayo

DEERBROOK EDITIONS

PUBLISHED BY

Deerbrook Editions
P.O. Box 542
Cumberland, ME 04021
www.deerbrookeditions.com
www.issuu.com/deerbrookeditions

FIRST EDITION

ISBN: 979-8-9865052-0-6

Book design by jeffrey Haste

Acknowledgements

"Illustrations by Author" first appeared in *Many Mountains Moving*, "Twice-Born World" and "Potter's Hovel" in *Hawaii Pacific Review*, "Rain Enough" in *Per Contra*, "You Will Be the Third One—" in *Prague Revue*, "Biography of a Gallstone" in *North American Review*, "Green Fire Ponds of Molėtai" in *Prism Magazine*, "The Deposition of Jadwiga Dobilas to the Military Delegation, 16 August 1834" in *Lituanus*, "Tongues" (as "Everybody Knows I Love My Toes") in *Words Literary Journal*, "Mother, His Own Mother" in *Stand Magazine*, "Scenes from a Green Bench in Vilnius" in *G.W. Review*, and "Blue" (as "The Blue Room") in *StoryQuarterly*.

Contents

One day teaches the other.

—Lithuanian proverb

Lithuania: Illustrations by Author

1. A char-black automobile, windows blown out. Bits of glass glitter in the sunlight.

2. A girl pokes her nose through diamond-shaped links of a metal fence. Her schoolmatescall her 'Vilkmergė,' girl who runs with wolves. She never speaks.

3. In a forest near Druskininkai one path becomes two paths.

4. A young woman in a small clearing picking wild strawberries.

5. Evening. An old woman, alone in a room. A candle burns near an amber-tinted photo of her husband, who wears the uniform of a partisan. She wonders: Will I go to communion?

6. The Dreamer of Dzūkija stands high above the side of the highway, just outside Merkinė. She wears the babushka, a plain shawl, and she is made of wood. Above her, in a wooden dream, the unicorn grazes.

7. This man is looking for the water closet. He goes through many doors of a barnyard, through pens of sheep, goats, pigs. He passes some chickens.

8. High reeds above the Šyša River. A heron glides through a scarlet sky.

9. The highway east of Merkinė. Wild poppies paint a field. A woman begs the driver to get on the bus to Kapčiamiestis.

10. A dog is barking in an abandoned amphitheater.

11. A man, standing at the main entrance of a day school. The strap of his satchel is looped over his left shoulder.

12. A woman soaks herself with a garden hose. The water-spray creates speckled rainbows. Twelve children are watching.

13. A boy has convinced his girlfriend to put her head inside the jaws of a large white dog. She does not feel the trickle of blood racing across her forehead.

14. Before sleep, the sacred Šventoji River scratches its back against a sandy bank.

15. At a kavinė. Two men shake hands and go to separate tables.

16. A young girl in a blue dress stands at the center of a large, empty, white room. She covers her eyes with her hands.

17. In Žemaitija a red stone rests upon a gray stone.

18. These two men stand outside a day school. One man has a satchel at his side. The other man is near a parked car. The door of the car is open.

19. Near Druskininkai, the cold, clear Ratnyčėlė flows. Across the stream, five white goats and one black bull.

20. This man was deported to Siberia.

21. The roebuck runs with the mare.

22. In a forest above a shallow ravine, a man is smoking, grieving for his son. Another man watches him from a distance. Later both men will meet at a kavinė. The man who watched the grieving man will say, "If I had known you and your son were Mafia I would not have become your friend."

23. In a forest near Druskininkai, two paths become one.

24. A footbridge over the Šventoji River collapses. A priest drowns. He was bringing communion bread to mass.

25. The waters of the confluence of the Merkys and Nemunas rivers. Alone in these waters, an island, where haystacks shimmer the late-day sun.

26 A man is trying to wrench a satchel free from another man's arm. The victim will fall to the ground and continue to clutch his satchel. His assailant will kick and punch him.

27. Black flies. In Siberia they will kill a human being after nine hours' exposure.

28. This girl runs to one corner of a large, empty room and tries to climb the wall. A woman enters the room carrying a pencil and paper. She holds the paper in front of the girl's face. The girl sits quietly on the floor and stares at the blank paper. The woman hands the pencil to the girl, who leans close to the page and writes her first word: "Why?"

29. In a forest near Vilnius, six paths converge where a shallow depression in the ground is filled with ashes. Close by, a rūta plant grows near a lost brown shoe, its toe-end slightly inclined on a rotting pine stump. Mosses have overgrown the tongue. A snail moves slowly to one of the eyelets.

—Darkness and swirling, undecided snow filled the meadow where our sheep wintered. Wind lashed my face as I approached them, their odd-shaped heads and round bodies weighted with wool dragging the ground. Through the flurries I saw a half-born lamb hanging from one mother's body. She waited for it to drop, her head lowered to the bitter wind. She would not let me near enough to help, and the half-born lamb hung in the wind so long the blood and mucus coating it turned to ice. It froze solid. After the first lamb froze and dropped, a second dropped straight down, steaming, alive. The mother licked it clean, took it quickly to her body on its shivering legs, and trotted off.

I returned to our house with the dead, frozen lamb and set it beside you while you slept, couldn't explain why, only knew that two lambs had fallen, one dead, one alive. With the snow still zigzagging in my head, I saw two versions of you, one alive and one dead, and two versions of myself.

—O Daughter, which version of you do I have before me now? How is it that you're here? Not some illusion?

—Your brother has felt himself go insane, and so he flies from Lithuania to New York.

—Your sister daydreams of marriage; she has grown three inches taller than me.

—Daughter, if you're here, and won't be going, then won't you stay? Won't you go this icy morning as you used to long ago, to our well, where the ground is blue in the dawn light, to heave on the long birch pole, to dip our cracked bucket inside until the frayed rope goes slack, until the bucket smacks the ice cap in the well, until you must heave again, up, down with all your strength, your feet leaving the ground, again and again, smacking the bucket against the ice, trying to get through . . .

—Won't you stay? But how can you knowing that once, in winter when we were starving, I thought of drowning you in my kitchen, but knew you would take hold of some pot handle or split ladle and live. I thought of burning you in the stove, but remembered the dizzying snow and the frozen lamb and knew your heart was icy and would not burn. So that spring, when you were too young to go into the forest alone, I sent you alone to pick mushrooms with my biggest basket. While you were gone, it rained so hard our stream swelled and I watched from the window for you to float by, out to sea, off, away, but you returned. When you came in the door your hair and clothes were perfectly dry and your basket was empty.

I asked, astonished, "How were you able to avoid the rain?"

"With the first drop, I took off all my clothes," you replied. "I put them under the mushroom basket. I stood under a nearby tree, the biggest and oldest by the lake. There was no time to find mushrooms."

"Go," I said, "back outside for the mushrooms. It's no use trying to trick me. You haven't even been in the forest. You're like your brother and sister. Talk! Talk! If I ripped their tongues out they would grow back instantly!"

—How? How is it that you're here, Daughter? And if you're here, then how is it that you are real? How is it that I now so easily forget this hard, hard winter and instead make a glorious summer. O Daughter, we ride! We fly the emerald sky! We climb upon the old hive our bees have abandoned, straddle it lightly, and with mighty laughter over the pea fields soar, then swoop low to pluck their papery flowers. Then we climb high, higher. We cleave the yellow moon! And when we return home we make a warm porridge and rub it under our armpits with great wooden spoons and become invisible and with giddy glee dance in the yard until the chickens go mad with their own clucking. At our gay command the huge birch stump fastened to the manger becomes a beautiful gray mare, and we mount her and fly again to the new, divided moon, where we meet an old man on one half of it.

"Do not milk your cow dry," he warns. "There will be nothing for the next day."

We laugh him in the face until he frowns. Oh, how the old man of the divided moon frowns! And, returning to earth, we milk our cow a hundred times over and fill our stomachs a hundred times full. We get out our broken boat, command it to float, then row to the place in Akmena Lake by the oldest and biggest tree, where cows stand in the shallow water. There, with our oars we churn butter from the water, roil hunks of it from the lake, all the while the cows moo and moo!

—O Daughter, then to the meadow we go, where we gather rūta, wild dill, and daisies. We weave wreaths of these for all the cows in the village and hang them about their huge, beautiful necks, skipping and singing, "Here are some black ones, and here are some brown ones, and here are some piebald ones!" Then the villagers come running out to see their cows, so beautiful, so transformed and shout, "But it's not Saint John's Day! How can it be?"

—If you're here, then fly with me, away on our magical mare, back home, home where you become a small carp flopping in our leaking trough and I a grain of barley in the mane of our mare. In the morning we make our invisible porridge again and sneak into your sister's wedding. We make ourselves so small we can hop into the mouths of her guests. We slide into their stomachs.

"I want something to drink!" I shout out their throats.

And you say, "I want something to eat!"

16

And they are astonished and silent and call the Priest back from the church to look down their throats, and lay his hands upon their Adam's apples and say words to drive us out.

"Words, words, words!" we giggle and fly out their mouths.

—O Daughter, if you're here, when we are truly thirsty, we land on Akmena Lake and, floating there on our beautiful mare, say to a man in his boat, "Here, use this worthless cracked ladle and scoop us out some water."

He stares at us with wonder, but he tries it and is amazed that not a drop spills.

When we are truly tired, we land on a sand beach and ask people there to make hemp from the sand—and they do! We make our hammocks in trees in the cool shade beyond the beach and rest as we have never rested.

And when our summer day grows old, we swoop into our chimney and sleep upon our warm stove, and if we don't like sleeping there well enough, we go into the leaking trough in the barn, fetch out two herring, harness them to the stove and command them to haul it out of the house and into the sky. They drop it in our frosted-over field of peas, where we may stoke it and sleep outdoors as warm as we please . . .

—O Daughter, how is it you're here? And if you're here, won't you stay? Won't you bring the cracked bucket that would not break the ice in our well, bring the split ladle from the hearth mantle? Won't you come with me when the night is cold and bright and spread with crystalline stars? Won't you follow me through the Rekalnis Forest, push with me through the bramble as if through the bristling winter fur of some strange animal? Won't you come along through the rustling and crackling and restless sounds in the hide of night to find the biggest and oldest tree, its roots spread into the lake like a dying hand? Won't you kneel where the water never freezes and fill the cracked bucket? O Daughter, won't you stay— and by the double light of the cleft and cowardly moon, we'll raise the split ladle to the cold, numb mouth of the twice-born world.

Rain Enough

When I arrived at the secondary school in the Administrator's grumble-storm of a village, he removed his brown-rimmed glasses and rubbed his eyes with two sharp knuckles. I took advantage of all his eye rubbing to pinch-wring water from my forehead. Water dribbled onto his office floor. When he stopped rubbing, eyes popped open above his slack-jowled, bull-doggish cheeks, I felt my stiff American smile roll up my face, then more water run off my upper lip and down my jawlines.

"Such groans of roaring wind and rain," the Administrator said, "I never remember to have heard." His quoting *King Lear* was not as astonishing as how good his English was and how he flaunted it.

"Yeah, it's a mess out there," I mumbled through a feeble baptismal smile.

"But you made it to Lithuania!" he said. "Now that the Soviets are gone, we are in need of native English speakers." He rose from his desk, and instructed me to leave my bags in the hall. "Besides, tonight is diskoteka!"

He snagged my arm and we left the school, huddled under his umbrella. We made straight for the nearby Cultural Center, so named because the new city government hadn't gotten around to changing the colorful Soviet nomenclature of civic buildings. Even so, he warned, some stubborn spe-cifics of culture held sway. Even in late summer, Lithuanians still dreaded the "draft disease," a mysterious condition brought upon by the slightest rumor of air moving in the room and, I expect, by people shivering in the wake of the Soviet natural gas embargo the winter of their declaration of independence.

He shook my hand and left me at a narrow doorway propped open with a small chunk of red brick. I entered amid bursts of cheap strobe light and digital techno-pounding while people ground themselves together, a kind of strange pelvic smooching in a relentless humid heat of bodies against nailed-shut windows. Water wouldn't know its place, its bullying cycle, solid, liquid, suffocating vapor. There was no escaping the stuff—and I blamed it; water was ruining my first time overseas, a volunteer, teaching English, my clear sense that I was doing something unsullied, unselfish.

Hand on waist, looking like a teacup, I wilted awhile by a wall, then decided to leave, when a young woman appeared, linked her arm in mine and lugged me toward a fibrous mass of cigarette smoke ensnaring frantic jutting elbows, heads, hands, all fetal kicking against what seemed the damp, cavernous interior of a giant cinderblock skull. Only my partner's luminous blue eyes seemed to penetrate the suffocating skein of dancers. Little spears of light glinted in them when the strobe fired. She was blond, thin, boy-bobbed hair. As she danced the straps of her blue-jean overalls popped up, down; her hips teeter-tottered in my hands. Soon she raised herself on tiptoe and ground against me with wider and wider oscillations of her hips. When I pushed her a little away, enough to make a centimeter or two of space between our reproductive organs, she didn't seem to mind, presumably because none of this pelvis-grinding was personal, something that degenerated into a kind of latch-as-latch-can frenzy, more like Brownian motion than romance, motion that made me, not usually aware of eighteenth-century sensibilities, long for gilded dance cards, wallflowers, perfumed handkerchiefs—and dry clothes.

But I liked the way her hips felt in my palms, undulating with the beat. But then she was at me again, grinding away at my fresh erection (which I'd begged to sit this one out!). She poked her tongue in my mouth and started to tickle the hard portion of my palate. At the same instant I felt her kick my pants cuff with the toe of her shoe, then her unshaven leg rasping against mine—and next realized I'd no air in my lungs; she'd drawn it all out! I began to panic; the techno-pounding seemed far away. Then we popped apart, pried so by two age-spotted hands, a thin woman with dark hair severely restrained by a large hairclip poking out her cranium as if part of the structure of her skull. She stood guard at the young woman's side, arms folded, staring crossly at me. My former dance-partner wiped her lips with the back of a hand, panted a couple times, and smiled.

"I'm Edward," I said to her, relieved by the duration of our separation.

Still out of breath, she pointed at her own sweat-beaded chest. "Lora," she said, then touched the elbow of the scowling older woman and added, "Jonė."

I started to say more—there had to be more to say in some language or other!—when Lora put her hand to her forehead.

"Atsiprašau—mano galvos"—her head, a headache, even I could salvage that much from my junkyard of Lithuanian words. Jonė took Lora's arm and guided her back into the sultry shadows of the Cultural Center.

Aroused and frightened by my encounter with Lora, I quickly left the diskoteka for my bags at the school. I entered the lobby and retrieved the key to my classroom from the Key Keeper. She was a large woman, the sort you see with their heads wrapped in babushkas, gold in their mouths, selling onions, carrots, and tomatoes in pails on sidewalks. For some reason the woman always seemed to have one button on the front of her gray smock unfastened, always a different one. As she handed my key to me, she glanced unexpectedly at the coat rack, as if someone were waiting to check a coat. I found the door, unlocked it, and stepped inside my classroom, its slate-colored walls and chalkboards so worn they shone alabaster. I removed teaching supplies and my umbrella from my suitcase, exited, and relocked the door.

When I returned my key to the Keeper, I navigated close to the coat rack and this time spotted her bottle of Stolichnaya poking out an old rubber boot. Once outside, I followed Kestučio Street northeast, toward the river and my lodgings at the Sonata Viešbutis, a way that took me through a neglected sculpture park made in Soviet times, gray granite statues scattered among stick-straight firs and peat, a collection of modern petroglyphs overgrown with broad, pale-green stands of fern: oversized snails and turtles mixed with full-size wolves and other forest creatures whose damp, blurred surfaces nearly overcame the essences of things they attempted to represent. The rain paused. I pressed a hand to a turtle's shell; its stone was cool and smooth, something beyond what the sculpture seemed to render. But more. I ran my fingers along its lichen-clotted grooves, soaked with rain, like the soggy lines in pine bark, tall blades of drenched grass, umbrageous, sodden canopies of birch and oak, and raspberry canes arcing out bushes like whips in restless wind.

The morning after my dance with Lora at the diskoteka I learned that she suffered a massive brain hemorrhage. Three days passed and she died in the Birštonas hospital, same place I'd been for my physical examination to teach. I hardly knew Lora. We hadn't even shared a language, just one sultry dance. Still, I scarcely believed she was dead, felt as if someone'd left a window open in my head—a draft rushed through—and I instantly recalled cats and chickens wandering the halls of the hospital where I'd waited alone for my physical. To die in a place where cats and chickens wandered. It was hard to imagine. How do you tell a story like that? One torrid dance. A miasma of wet rasping fabric and skin. Wandering cats and chickens. A young woman gone, so suddenly.

When I entered the Administrator's office, he'd hiked his glasses to his forehead, and was pinching the bridge of his nose, so industriously I wondered if he'd been crying, for Lora, I assumed.

"For the rain it raineth every day," he said, then gingerly settled his glasses on his nose, seeming satisfied to show off his *Twelfth Night*. "Lora's funeral is this afternoon," he added. "You are excused from your duties to attend."

"Thank you, but I'm just getting to know my students, and—"

"Lora's aunt, Jonė, teaches mathematics here," he said. "She has invited a few colleagues." His voice stiffened and his face flushed, leaving pools of white at his cheeks. "You should go."

I'd been overseas just enough to know to be endlessly open-minded about these matters.

"Alright," I said, "but I didn't know her well."

The Administrator told me that Lora came to live with her aunt Jonė after Lora's parents were killed in a train accident. Both women lived quite alone in a small cabin a little west of the sculpture park. They kept to themselves, so much so the Administrator was surprised to hear that Lora had been to the diskoteka. He went on to say that since Jonė appeared at the dance, it could only be to fetch Lora home early.

"Now," the Administrator smiled. "You know Lora."

Lora was buried in a warm September rain at the cemetery east of the center of Birštonas, her grave hidden from the road by brooding deep-green poplars that reached half-over an iron gate and quaked as if accusing her resting place of not having quite enough shade. It was through such a strange untended place mourners passed from church to burial site, where Lora's freshly varnished, closed coffin sat next to a hole freshly dug and a mound of earth, curiously shaped like a pair of shoulders without a head. Two gravediggers stood by, leaning on their shovels. After a time, the headless shoulders near Lora's open grave slicked over with drizzle and seemed to melt. I could not find the Administrator anywhere, but remember his mourning instructions as I left his office.

"You stand at attention," he said, "and see nothing with your eyes."

It rained harder. Umbrellas went up, and I suddenly found Lora's aunt Jonė with me under my umbrella. She wore a black mourning dress with a high lace collar, along with the customary black sash running diagonally across her chest and hip. She floated next to me and hovered, giving me one of those, "Young man, you don't mind, do you?" line-smiles I'd gotten from other women my senior on trans-Atlantic flights: "Young man, you don't mind if I put my extra bag under your foot rest, do you?" She leaned a little toward me, close enough to detect her heavy perfume, honeysuckle, and she stood, stiff-straight. This stiff-standing, stone silence went on a long time among the mourners.

I was the only person not wearing a black sash. Other mourners appeared to be cleft by the black gaps of grief running across their bodies. Their muscles assumed a kind of living rigor one only expects after death. I kept thinking their features would melt away in the ruinous rain, starting from the tips of their umbrellas, the way time acts on ancient statues, but they stood, whole, stolid, cuffs and shoes soaked dark, like the soaked petroglyphs I'd seen in the sculpture park. Lithuanian words drifted through the damp air. I started faking Lithuanian words to a hymn, sounding them out, hoping to blend in. After a time, failing to sound words out, I spotted a young blond woman with a splendidly expressive mouth, her eyes closed in fervent grief, and made with my mouth the shapes of words she made with hers; all this I imitated, until the third hymn, when the young woman's eyelids suddenly sprung open, like day upon night, startled me, and I had to stop mouthing words. I went back to piecing them out by sound alone, which also failed, and I was left with my silence and the drumbeat of raindrops on the fabric of my umbrella.

Lora's wake was a little after the burial, at the Nemuno Viešbutis, a sagging structure south of the sculpture park, three stories, painted a peeling, dull, greenish yellow, its eaves and balconies dripping with intricate, dirty white fretwork, like unwashed lace. Once inside, we all observed our silent staring awhile, then took breaks from it to obediently consume hunks of bee-comb oozing with honey, accompanied by wild raspberries threaded onto stiff stalks of wild grass. The food was spread on a long table covered with a red-checkered cloth. Just as I reached for a dish of honeycomb, the cloth bunched against the side of the plate, and I found the Administrator at my elbow, his voice behind me.

"Do you see that wrinkle in the tablecloth?" he whispered. "The belief is that wrinkle is a ghost clutching the cloth, trying to get at the food."

I was glad to hear a whistle of English in the maelstrom of Lithuanian. But the entire time the Administrator spoke, I dared not turn around. It was like he was the clinging ghost himself.

"Interesting," I said, and reached for a chunk of fresh honeycomb, but before my fingers found the sweet, sticky, clover-scented stuff, the Administrator went on.

"If you take a bit of food intended for the ghost, it will attach itself to you and follow you about, hungry, clinging for years."

My appetite for honeycomb vanished. I quickly shoved the dish aside, smoothed the cloth, and turned to face the Administrator, who had vanished as well.

After a time, most mourners in the room were quite skilled at maintaining their empty gazes while smoothly guiding food into their mouths. Their curious manner of repast restored my appetite. After a while I could ably guide a stalk of wild raspberries into my mouth without revealing even a shred of joy in its taste, all the while maintaining an appropriate far-off gaze of grief, this, partly assisted by a trick I learned: I would stare with blank astonishment, my mouth part open, upon strips of garish red wallpaper that had separated from the wall and hung like wet tongues uncoiled in the room.

A little later, Jonė began an impromptu eulogy, of which I could only follow small parts, words such as "vaikas," "child"; "laukti," "wait"; and the obligatory "Dievo," "God." Jonė's body language was even less revealing: She stood stiff-straight behind a crooked music stand, eyes glazed, nose tilted slightly upward at the ceiling light. A fly desperately zigzagged about a single bare bulb, something that reminded me of diskoteka-dancing with Lora only a few days before.

After the wake, I strolled awhile in the sculpture park before returning to my room at the Sonata. The rain had slowed and damp conifers scented the air. The wind stiffened and brought up goose-bumps along my arms. I felt awake, alert—alive. Then behind me I heard Jonė clop-clopping in her wooden heels, along the narrow asphalt walk choked with morning glory and weeds, navigating her way through the petroglyphs. Her hairclip sailed above her head. The black furls of her mourning dress filled with wind and floated behind her in pillows of black.

"Palauk!" she cried.

I slowed and she caught me. She gathered up her dark pillows and smoothed them out of sight.

She clopped up to my side, line-smiled. A metal-green scarab light glinted in her eyes. I tried to fold up my umbrella quickly, but she ducked under it quickly. She looked at me in a way I knew she had very little English; her eyes wobbled in her head, searching for mine, until she seemed to decide she'd locked onto them. Then she looped her arm inside mine, clutching, so tightly it seemed the whole of her personage attached to me. This, in turn, was not so strange as walking in utter silence in her damp ravenesque presence.

I tried to form a Lithuanian phrase to express my surprise and discomfort, said, "Nesuprantu"—"I don't understand," the best I could come up with, but nothing seemed up to the task of separating her from me, other than physical repulsion, which I considered, but then we were at the portico of the school and I dashed inside, saying something like, "Man rekia mano kynygai"—I need my books—and I did!

Morning, I found myself staring down from my viešbutis window to the remnants of Lenin's statue, two pant legs cut off at the knees. Then I saw Jonė stroll up, still in mourning clothes. She sat on the stump of one of Lenin's knees, and gazed up at my window, rain slicking her hair into a coal-black stone. I was convinced she was making herself look wet and miserable, a ruse to insure I would share my umbrella with her on the way to school. I quickly stashed my umbrella in my closet and headed for the back entrance of the building, knowing I'd be soaked by the time I reached the school, but worth it to walk gloriously alone!

I descended in the world's slowest lift, whose shaft brought close to ear a cacophony of voices on other floors waiting for it to arrive. I dashed for the Key Keeper's desk, leaving her with an astonished "O" shape of mouth as I sped by, my room key appearing in her hand as if magic. I put my shoulder to the back door and forced it open. And there stood Jonė, wet, arms folded over her black sash. Her perfume that now smelled old and vinegary. Her line-smile had become a wrinkled pout.

I rolled my eyes skyward, shrugged to indicate I had no umbrella to offer her, hoping she would clop over to one of the other teachers to share an umbrella, but no! She produced an umbrella of her own, and danced to my side as if a second's hesitation might permit one more fatal drop of rain to strike my head. Again we strolled silently to the school, a tug of war. If I sped up, she let out a tiny yelp like a wounded puppy until I slowed, and clutched my arm even tighter.

Once inside the school, she closed her umbrella and shook it. I seized the moment, bolted to the Administrator's office, and found him there, his eyeglasses stuck to his forehead and eyes closed.

"Ka?" he said, eyes shut, then, "what?" when he recognized me.

"I think Jonė has the wrong idea about my attending Lora's funeral. She's becoming, well, attached."

He worked his glasses over his eyes and seemed to search for mine a few seconds.

"Maybe she is only grieving."

"Grieving? I don't know her!"

"Alright," he said. "I will tell her not to become attached to you. Is that correct?"

"Alright," I replied and swayed side to side nervously, a motion he followed with his eyes until they swam and refocused.

"Don't worry," he said. "I'll interpret for you. We need you!"

I made my way to my classroom, cautiously relieved that the Administrator had promised to talk to Jonė, when a new fleet of raindrops smacked the windows of the building, the beginning of another drenching, setting metal eaves to ringing, articulate, talkative, yet incomprehensible.

When I reached the lobby to fetch my classroom key, the Key Keeper was curiously absent, the lobby transformed into a tropical zone: the atmosphere damp, musty, fed by four small waterfalls pouring out holes in the ceiling, one in each quadrant of the hapless room. Finding the lobby utterly empty, I went into the basement in search of the Key Keeper only to find water cascading from the lobby, through the floor, and splashing into rust-colored divots in the cement. A cold steam arose from the base of the waterfalls and filled the basement with an unrelenting fog. I ran my hand through one cold stream, felt the upsplash on my face, then heard the Key Keeper's chair scud on the floor above. I went back upstairs, past the Administrator's office, and saw him speaking with Jonė through the partially open door. The Key Keeper had reinstalled herself in her booth near the coat check room, and she'd spotted four yellow garbage pails under the four waterfalls. Two were running over and two leaking out the bottoms. Still, inspired by the sight of the Administrator's meeting with

Jonė, and somehow wanting a cheerful word to overcome so much water, I blurted to the Key Keeper, "Labadiena!"

She crossed her arms over her chest, shook her head. "Ka?"

I knew she understood my word. What was so complicated about 'Good day?'

I tried another word.

"Lietus," I said, holding my palm out, as if rain were falling into it, and waiting for my key. I thought commiserating over the watery weather might strike some note of empathy in the Key Keeper. But she smiled painfully, as if I were Typhoid Mary, dragged open her drawer of keys, picked out mine, then let it dangle over my palm two-three seconds before ceremoniously letting it drop.

When school let out, the sun suddenly blazed forth, a sign, I was sure, that days ahead would be brighter. So touched by light, I made my way to Saint Antano's tiny cathedral east of the school near the river, a special service to remember two Birštonas partisans, "Forest Sisters," who resisted to their deaths the Soviet occupation just after World War Two. The gaunt, three-steepled cathedral sat drying in the sun, its red brick still blotched with a week's worth of rainstorm. On its old wooden altar sat a large black-and-white photograph of the sisters, taken deep in a pine forest. The two young women gazed directly into the camera lens, one, blond, reclining behind what looked like a Browning Automatic Rifle complete with bipod, her right arm resting so naturally along the thigh of one leg she might have been a Botticelli in battle fatigues. Next to her knelt a dark-haired woman with Mona Lisan countenance. A grenade launcher hung by a black leather strap dividing her chest. Pines surrounded both women completely, needles at their feet, fronds and cones above, lush forest all around.

I felt water hit my face and turned to the aisle to see a priest dip a large willow switch into a pail, cock it over one shoulder, and catapult holy water an incredible distance down the nave to rat-tat-tat on the back wall. A cloud suddenly uncovered the sun and a stained glass window poured a rainbow near my pew. I thought: baptized a second time, first in rain, now in sun?

When I exited the cathedral, Birštonas took on a new depth; sunlight seemed to illuminate and penetrate everything—a row of dill weed gone to seed, vibrating in the breeze; a hay wagon broken down in the main road; and farther in the distance a stork's nest atop a power pole, its twigs and branches poking into blue sky. Far into the pines, trunks were bruised damp-brown from rain. I was elated. So, upon seeing Jonė at the base of the cathedral steps, and knowing the Administrator has spoken to her, I shouted, "Labas, Jonė!"

She arranged the clip in her hair a bit, wriggled a little in her mourning dress, not black in sunlight, but now seeming a shade of deep metallic purple. She handed me a postcard of Basanavičius's statue in the town center, a leader in educational reform in Lithuania, whose beard growing high on his face made him appear hermit-like. The card read, in her hand, 'With beast wishes, Jonė.'

I laughed, admit I felt touched by her 'beast.' So I asked, "Do you want English lessons?"

"Ne!" She nodded vigorously in the direction of the river.

"Okay," I said, "Nemunas."

Once more we walked in silence, now without aid of an umbrella, no arm-latching as before. We passed long, hive-like sanatoria, then came to a broad pedestrian-only walk through thick pines. She peddled forward on her own, a little ahead, careful to not let me out of her shadow. We neared thick bulrushes at the riverbank. Jonė kicked off her heels, carried them by their back straps in one hand, swung them like a schoolgirl, head back bathing her mourning face in the sun. I slowed near the river's edge, knowing we were close to water. I dreaded being that close to the river, especially knowing how high it had risen in the past few days, yet Jonė forged ahead, until, suddenly, the mighty Nemunas lay before us, current scouring its sides like an enormous blue-green snake, sunlight glancing off its scales. I could feel it ready to coil about me in cold, constricting intimacy. Jonė laughed, snagged my hand to balance herself, then walked into the swift water to her waist. I stumbled forward—and plunged into waist-deep river with her! Jonė's mourning dress billowed about me. I began to beat the dark fabric down, but, rather than rescue herself, she clamped both arms about my waist, the terrible cloth still looming. I slogged toward to the riverbank, Jonė clinging the whole time, her sopped black satin trailing in the bulrushes. I attempted to pull her arms from my waist, but she resisted.

"Lora!" she shouted.

I pried her from me and left her lying on the riverbank.

When I arrived at school the next morning, I went straight to the Administrator's office.

"How do you like our fine Lithuanian sunshine?" he asked.

"It's nice," I replied.

"So, how is it going with Jonė?"

"Not well. I don't want her near me."

He took up a pocketknife and began sharpening a pencil.

"How near?"

"Near enough for physical contact."

"What kind of contact?"

"Close contact!" I blurted. "Very close contact!"

I left his office, had to get to my classroom. The school day seemed long, longer than the rainiest days ever seemed. My students, an affable group to be sure, had little to do with it. Nor did my anticipation of basking in the new sunlight when school let out. When the final bell rang, my students left, and the Administrator entered my classroom.

His face was a collage—bright red nose and neck in contrast to pasty-white jowls—yet he spoke cheerfully.

"I have solved your problem with close contact."

"Thank you," I replied, looking straight at him yet seeing nothing, the same advice he'd given me for Lora's funeral. "I hope you did not hurt Jonė's feelings."

"Too late. The huyrly-burly's done!" He reached into his front pants pockets with both hands and rocked a little on his heels. "I have discharged Jonė."

"Discharged?"

"Of course. I told her she is a disgrace to our school and to her country."

"Her country? You didn't need to fire her!"

"Let's forget it," he said with a dogged smile. "We need you. I promise, tomorrow will be different."

When I left the Administrator's office, I headed for the Sonata. When I reached it, I could not bear to return to my room. I took the lift alone two-three times, heard sounds of other teachers echo in the elevator shaft, and felt I'd failed my first and only time away from home.

In the coming weeks, I visited the Sculpture Park. The sun had yet to relent. Everything dried out. Pale conifers dry-chaffed above, wild raspberry bushes brooded, their droughty branches heavy with late-summer fruit. When I entered the Park, once rich dark lines of petroglyphs were bone dry, washed faint with bright light. My turtle had become only turtle and no more. The cantankerous sounds of rain and twangling eaves of the school only memories. My once stygian and watered world seemed a dream in someone else's skies. Rain enough, and the world wanted sun; enough sun, and it now longed for rain to return.

I turned to the cemetery where Lora rested under poplars that reached half over the iron fence, leaving half sun, half shade, where, over poplars, blackbirds flocked to limb, unflocked, spiraled out to pock the cloudless azure sky.

"Lora," I whispered, as if needing desperately to hear my voice in a place of such silence. Then, "Jonė" when I realized I was utterly alone.

Beyond the cemetery, there was a bend in the road I'd never noticed.

I watched and waited.

You Will Be the Third One—

So the name of the old-town tavern, "Būsi Trečias," means in English, where I waited for you in Vilnius, accompanied only by the tavern's disputatious owner, our two faces into tankards of mead, a weird yellow light bathing us, cast by a dust-coated bulb above the bar. Tables, chairs, ceiling beams all glowed a torpid amber, seemed antediluvian, though I suspected in full light such appointments may prove fake.

"I am expecting someone," I told the Owner.

He glanced about the empty tavern.

"A third?" he laughed. "Sure you are."

I explained you were late, didn't know by how much, the mead you know, but the Owner lifted his young face from his tankard, walked his fingers through red stubble, then took up a cracked brass hand bell and shook it once, a peal that resonated the length of his bony wrist then fell dead in air.

"You ring that bell with each draught?" I asked.

He filled our tankards with mead again, so high I swear meniscuses brimmed far over our rims. I handed him another twenty litai.

"I announce that I'm pouring. Is it my fault you are my only customer? I'll ring it again when your third arrives—*if* he arrives."

"She," I said.

He was very self-satisfied with his prying such a personal pronoun from me, and continued to insinuate you'd not arrive as we'd agreed.

For a time I didn't reveal anything more to my interrogator. But it was mead—old honey vapor—that tickled my lips, rose to numb my ear tips, and carried me back to you, our little journey by automobile earlier that afternoon. Do you remember? I'm afraid I bored the Owner of Būsi Trečias with details, how we rumbled up Gedimino prospektas in your new Fiat, among a bevy of other tremulous, imported machines, past two brooding Soviet ghosts, one a Lada, another a Moskvich, our little flock flying down a line of parked cars so close you set off one's alarm, then another's, so both cars blurted their high-tech affronts in strange syncopation, as if at long last trumpeting in the blush and blossom of full spring after eons of Lithuanian winter.

"You are a terrible driver," I said, that crazy heraldic trumpeting receding.

"Am I so very terrible?"

We nearly sideswiped a red ledai cart and I imagined death by ice cream, one of syrupy white emulsion coating my face, flecked with crushed hazelnuts.

"I simply do not wish to die stupidly, that's all."

You slowed down, crawled actually, while a chorus of car horns yacked behind us.

"Alright," you huffed, "if I slow up, will you please stay another year with us on your Fulbright? It is hard to find native speakers suitable for the Department of English Philology. After all, it is *English* philology!"

I examined then removed my white knuckles from your dashboard.

"You're Chair. You are required to ask me to stay, aren't you?"

A tepid breeze blubbered through your open window, mussing your hair, blond and streaked steel-gray; you stroked and guided a twisted, errant lock from your mouth and hooked it behind an ear—then removed both hands from the steering wheel to snag other ungovernable locks and tuck them behind both ears, all of which resulted in our drifting close to another vehicle, whose velocity and trajectory compounded my fear since it seemed as misguided as ours!

You re-stuck your hands to the wheel at the last possible moment before impact, jerked left.

"But really, why won't you stay?" you persisted. "Is life so much better in America?"

I lied: "I must go back. I am missed by my wife."

"That is a peculiar way to say it," you said, stomped the brake, fishtailed right onto Vytauto gatvė, squeezed your way through two mini-vans, then completed a screeching left onto Latvių, heading for a scrim of pines on a ridge in the west overlooking Vilnius, the far side of Karoliniškių Park, where you lived.

"How is it peculiar?" I said.

"I mean the passive voice," you laughed. "You said, 'I am missed by my wife.' Is it really the same as 'My wife misses me?'"

I paused in my account of our automotive adventure and sipped on my mead.

"And?" the Owner of Būsi Trečias asked. "I assume you arrived safely at this woman's place?"

"Yes."

And there was more. But I told the Owner he would not be interested.

"Probably not," he said, then drew on his tankard, hard and proper, as if each millisecond his lips contacted the sweet mead was necessary for optimal satisfaction. No more. No less.

"I suppose you can tell a better story?"

I startled myself a little by challenging the Owner. It seemed that after living a year in Lithuania, I'd gotten past my whatever-natives-of-the-

country-say-is-okay syndrome. Perhaps you've noticed? Anyway, he set his
tankard down, went in back, and returned with a white brick of kiaules—
smoked pig lard; he smeared a hunk onto a piece of black bread and
offered it to me. A clever diversion, but I wasn't biting. I took the kiaules,
set it aside, stuck my elbows to the old oak bar, fist under chin, and waited
for the Owner to begin his story.

After World War Two, my grandfather was a partisan, one of thousands
who fled into the forests after the Soviet occupation of Lithuania in 1944.
He lived in the forests around Biržai, far north of here, where lakes are
cold, clear, pines thick and tall. That summer, he went into villages for
food and supplies and slept in the forest with six other partisans. But then
in late summer he and a man named Liudvikas decided to build a bunker
into a hillside over the Nemunėlis River, a place to winter, and a kind of
resistance headquarters. They had to build their bunker large enough to
accommodate seven men and deep enough to conceal it from Red Army
soldiers, NKGB, and Stribai—Soviet collaborators
"Stalin's hounds," Liudvikas called these Stribai, and when other par-
tisans groaned about the enormous task of building the bunker, added,
"You must give your fatherland all that you are obliged to!"
These were good men, patriots, but they may not have taken a man
like Liudvikas seriously. Before the war, he'd been a part-time carpenter
and full-time fixture at local pubs. But when he entered the forest with
other partisans, it transformed him. One day, my grandfather happened
upon Liudvikas leaning on a birch tree, cleaning his rifle, with two hawks
perched on his shoulders, a strange kind of trinity my grandfather never
forgot, and one he'd never witness again. After that, he could never think
of Liudvikas in the same way.
So these seven men built their bunker in the forest, overall shaped like
an "L," 12 meters by 12 meters square. They cut and hewed pine trees
and fashioned 2.2 meter high walls. At the terminus of one leg of the "L"
they made an entrance and two-seat latrine, at the opposite end a sleeping
room, complete with a vent to the surface to supply air.
In the sleeping room, Liudvikas led meetings of the partisans. He talked
a lot about the Stribai, with a bitter warmness in his voice.
"We are only disarming our countrymen who have confused their loy-
alty to Lithuania with loyalty to the Soviet Union."
But all the men knew that "disarm" meant "kill."
That winter, the seven partisans were warm enough as they went about
planning the business of disarming our country's foes. They scouted daily
but found no sign of the occupiers or their vile collaborators. The summer
that followed was suffocating. The air passage to the surface ended at the

base of a pine, protected by a wire screen that was often covered by falling pine needles, leaves, and debris. The men complained about clearing it daily. At times the boiling heat was so intense the men could not stay inside the bunker at all. Worst of all, a kind of black fungus grew on the walls and floor and the spores set several of the men to coughing constantly. A damp, earthy atmosphere surrounded everything, so much so that most of the time the men preferred to take their chances in the open forest.

I imagine Lithuanians have many stories of the Soviet occupation. So you understand—eventually, the Owner of Būsi Trečias became bored with his own narrative. Even as he drank from his tankard, he seemed to imbibe the same boredom that his grandfather and Liudvikas felt as they went day-to-day unsuccessfully scouting for Red soldiers or Stribai.

"There were simply none to be found in such a remote location," he explained.

The Owner sipped his mead, settling forward a bit, a strange posture, as if his muscles had involuntarily become more cynical than he wanted them to be. Then he sank back. When I pinched the black bread slathered with kiaules and spun it a couple times, he seemed to become animated, but then slipped back into lethargy, and so I continued to relate to him the doleful details of my day with you, hoping he'd see how much more exciting his story had been to someone like me, and encourage him to continue.

Naturally, I told him your name, don't know why I'd left it out, and how you brought your Fiat to a scuffing halt at the end of a red-mud drive. You got out, blew another strand of ropy hair from your face, and smoothed your skirt over your thighs. You were really tricked out—forest green wool skirt, black silk blouse. You went into the back seat and retrieved a two-handled shopping bag, some end-of-the-school-year gifts for teachers in the Department. You clip-clopped to your door and fumbled for a key in your faux Gadino handbag. Only then did I exit your terror machine, taking no small degree of satisfaction in hearing its death rattle as the engine cooled and ticked among the pines. I followed you inside hesitantly, nothing personal, but I was sure you would use the occasion of this party to publicly pressure me to stay in Lithuania. I entered your new, smoked glass A-frame, resented your backward glances as you went into the foyer, little warnings, I was certain, that the real struggle for my staying in your country was about to begin. My knees went weak, mind sunk into that past winter's knee-deep, ice-crusted snow on impossibly inclined Naugarduko gatvė, how several times a week I slogged the great distance from my flat on Savičiaus up Naugarduko's inhuman hill for food and supplies. Then I remembered how one time school kids on a high floor of the secondary school overlooking Naugarduko began flinging water balloons and water-filled soda bottles out the windows at passersby on the sidewalk below. One old man finally shook his fist and shouted:

"Ungrateful brats! Shame! You are all a disgrace to our fatherland!"

He kept shaking his fist until a two-liter bottle landed on his chest, toppling him

to the walk, half-burying him in the stinging snow. Suddenly, the windows of the high floor snapped shut and a teacher slip-slid out the main door. She helped the old man to his feet and hurried him inside the school building, not so much out of compassion as embarrassment.

I shook off the cold of the past winter when you introduced me to your husband, a German national who soon left us for a far part of the house. You revealed that your husband was a salesman, traveling throughout Europe, selling wine, not Lithuanian wine, just wine of some sort or other for some European country or other. A little later, after you'd left a glass of his red mystery wine in my hand, I saw where your husband had gotten to, spied him through your French doors, on the Tuscan-tiled patio, under a Chinese elm, overrun with wild English roses. There he was, synchronously pacing, back and forth, the width of the patio with the largest, blackest German shepherd I'd ever seen, an animal that seemed to come to your husband's chest. In large measure, the conjuncture of man and dog scared me. I knew I was unwanted, their ritual private. But in small measure, I felt sorry for them as they paced back and forth, so bored, so constrained, commiserating over the geometry of their incarceration on the patio. After a time they took to pacing the diagonal of the patio, extracting all the freedom they could from the additional centimeters the hypotenuse afforded them.

You see, I think it was your husband's pacing with the Shepherd that got the Owner going again on his narrative. Eventually, realizing that their plans to disarm the occupiers were going nowhere, five of the men decided to broaden their scouting and join other partisan groups, south, in the Dzukija region . . .

As I said, Liudvikas had been a carpenter before a partisan. My grandfather studied architecture at Vytautas Magnus University. Both men had invested quite a bit in the design and construction of the bunker. And they believed the occupiers would soon present themselves to be disarmed. So the remainder of that first summer, only my grandfather and Liudvikas stayed behind to mind the bunker. My grandfather set a typewriter on a stump outside the bunker. He occupied his time typing a newsletter that he distributed weekly in nearby villages, where he also collected news of the resistance. All copies had to be typed from scratch, but he was quite comfortable. The forest floor was spongy with mosses. He sat at the stump, wrapped his legs about it, and typed, sometimes feeling the stump and typewriter were the only things he could cling to in the turning, tumultuous world. He worked many hours like this in the shade of nearby alders. But sometimes, hearing the echoic tapping of the machine's keys in the forest mesmerized him more than the content of his words; he stopped typing, dumbstruck by the incongruity of the machine, its dire mechanical duty, and the natural beauty of the forest, especially near dusk, when his memories of before the war and resistance broke surface. From the hill into which they'd built the bunker, he could see a long way, could see workhorses, some lazing in meadows, others standing by hay wagons near fields of blossoming rye. Beyond this, the Nemunėlis wound through tufts of willow and bulrushes, while two hawks glided overhead. Such vistas in dying sunlight created his mood, but a desire rose in him, unbound by the mood, clear and painful; he wanted to study again; he missed university life, wanted something more, but then his desire subsided, and he reached down assure himself his Czech ZB-26 machine gun rested ready against his leg. His spirit sank with its familiar touch. He felt like an old clock winding down, one on which the world somehow depended. So he reached back, again sought the typewriter's keys with his fingertips, and typed, knowing the necessity of the machine in the forest, its reality, this third thing existing with the two men and their forest hideaway.

Far from such complicated emotions, Liudvikas simply hated my grandfather's typewriter. While my grandfather typed, Liudvikas squatted near my grandfather with the butt of the Sturmgewehr rifle planted between his knees to balance him. Liudvikas's mother had given him the Sturmgewehr the same night the Red Army entered Vilnius. She and Liudvikas's father had resisted the occupation. Liudvikas watched his mother run over rooftops to escape; his father was less lucky, running through the woods, fatally wounded, his shirt on fire.

"If you must bang away on that thing," he said, "take it into the bunker."

My grandfather paused, looked at Liudvikas, and turned his palms up.

"I need the light," he replied, shrugged, and continued typing.

"Then just stop and listen!" Liudvikas commanded. "I have learned that in Spalviškiai there is a stribas who informed on Giedrius last winter."

"Are you sure?"

"My old friend Žigimantas was sure. And he saw this stribas remove a Lithuanian flag from his own rooftop!"

The Owner was slowing up on his mead, and I believe he paused here to collect himself to get the next installment of his story right.

He shook the cracked bell once. I reached to cover my tankard but he slopped more mead inside. I gasped; he laughed.

I hope you know I would not have told him the rest of our story, but when he rang that bell, it sounded like he'd won a round of boxing. So I went on with our narrative, wanting to top his adventurous story, knowing it to be hopeless, but continued anyway, how more of our colleagues arrived at your party—Aurelija, who said that my "lazy" students did not deserve the pizza I'd bought them last week; Ona, who seemed eternally nonplussed when I declined to attend her dying husband's birthday party; Petras, who continued to call me Yank, when I'd informed him I hated the expression; and Zivilė, who'd offered me her months-late condolences at the 9/11 attack on World Trade Center, finishing with, "So, like Lithuania, you now know what it feels like to be attacked on your own soil."

Only when our little group went through to the patio did your husband stop his pacing with the German shepherd. He smiled, as if we'd all rescued him, then went back into the house, leaving the massive canine alone on its haunches. As each new guest strolled onto the stone tiles, the beast dipped its head in a kind of polite yet menacing nod, as if making some sort of terrible tally.

I asked you for a refill, and you complied. When you returned, I took the glass of wine and said, "I hope you will not use this party as an occasion to publicly beg me to stay."

"Of course I will."

"And if I still refuse to stay?"

"Then I will meet you tonight at Būsi Trečias."

"I'd like that, but there's really no point."

The Shepherd was watching us both. I eyed him back a moment, then commented on the size of the brute, to which you replied, "I keep him for protection. My husband uses him for companionship. So it all works for the best." I eyed the beast again. He dipped his head lowest of all; his yellow eyes half-rolled up into his head and he considered me. "Now," you added, "you were saying?"

"Never mind," I replied, unlatched my gaze from the creature, and retreated.

I nudged my way across the patio, near the French doors. I figured should you start your speech to our colleagues, I could drift off to the loo and spare myself the embarrassment. But before I could depart, you appointed yourself at the center tile of the patio, by your silent posture alone quieted our colleagues, and found a home for yet another errant lock of hair behind an ear. You began making the usual addresses, something about spring and our thawing emotions, our parting, the magic of oncoming summer, and then, "I am sad to announce that," at which point

I knew you'd reveal my decision to depart to everyone. I turned my eyes to the patio tiles, then up again to catch those of the Shepherd, which, rather than staring into mine, glanced away to you, bolted forward, gripped your right leg in his forelegs, and unceremoniously began to hump it, all the while you tried, again and again, to ignore the beast nearly toppling you, saying, "I'm sad to," "I'm so sad," "I'm devastated," each utterance followed by a wave of canine passion thrusting, jerking your hip left, left, left—all this in total silence as our colleagues stared, not trying to help, I myself conflicted since removing the lascivious beast from your leg likely meant you'd continue with your embarrassing speech designed to make me stay. So I—we—all waited for you to drag the reluctant creature across the patio, limp through the French doors and into the kitchen, where we heard the crinkle of a bag of dog treats, the spatter of kibbles against the wall, a sigh of relief, and, after a few moments during which I assumed you composed yourself, you returned, more red mystery wine from some European country or other in hand, smiling, chatting, abandoning the dolorous announcement about my departure altogether.

I told the Owner it was unlikely that you would join us, be our third. I said I had to believe the carnal encounter with the Shepherd had sapped your willpower, your persistence in asking me to stay in Lithuania. I told the Owner this with sadness in my voice, for I would miss you, your reckless driving, frenetic hair, your animal magnetism! But the Owner failed to reply, other than to ring his hand bell once. I tried to break the pattern, the dead peal of the cracked bell, his insistent re-pouring. I wanted him to stop. I took up the bit of black bread smothered with kiaules and complied with the Owner's earlier invitation, felt the pasty white smoke coat my tongue, hoped my gesture would begin some new pattern. But he simply dribbled more mead into my tankard and continued his story...

My grandfather knew the story, how the Soviets left the corpse of Giedrius near the old courtyard in Spalviškiai, naked, stiff, bloated, a warning to citizens nailed on a fencepost that no one was permitted to touch or remove the body on pain of arrest—and that which would surely follow arrest. Only Žigimantas, the town drunk, drunk, of course, wandered close enough to report that three pins were driven into the corpse's left eyelid, the scrotum torn open, both testicles removed, and so many blunt-force bruises to the torso that, taken as a whole, it looked uniformly purplish yellow. When the Red Army soldiers ran the drunk off, he reported later to Liudvikas that he heard one soldier say, "And there are more traitors we know of, thanks to—" and this is where Žigimantas slurred something like "Algimantis"—or "Algimas"—or "Algis," all three names possessed by three men in town, two of whom Liudvikas knew, declared to be patriots, and the third, Algis, a man who notoriously kept to himself at the edge of the forest in a ramshackle stone hut.

So Liudvikas and my grandfather set off for the stone hut outside of Spalviškiai. They found it near dusk, a faint red glow of light in the front window, deep-throated bullfrogs bleating all around. Both men rested their weapons either side of the doorframe. Liudvikas knocked and, Algis, a small, red-bearded man opened the door.

"I'm busy," Algis said, his voice flat, matter-of-fact, almost as if he expected the two men to visit him, though he obviously knew neither.

Liudvikas now believed it was "Algis" he'd heard Žigimantas slur earlier that day. He glanced at my grandfather, took up his Sturmgewehr, and shoved the barrel against Algis's chest with such force the man toppled backwards onto his plank floor.

Algis rose slightly to rest on his elbows and stared up at Liudvikas, rather like a schoolboy who'd been knocked flat in a fist fight, grimacing, but without surprise, another sign that Liudvikas took for Algis's guilt.

"You're a dirty stribas!" Liudvikas said. "We've come to disarm you in the name of the Lithuanian Freedom Army."

My grandfather began to search the hut for weapons, first pulling a dozen or so books from a pine bookcase behind the man's elbows.

"I don't have any arms," Algis said, then smiled, knowing he'd been holding his bodily arms out, palms up, in a gesture of proof that he had no 'arms,' a smile that seemed to further infuriate Liudvikas.

"We know you have a weapon," Liudvikas grinned. "Your big mouth!"

"Algis rose a little on one elbow, said, "I'm a poet. I don't take sides. I don't talk to anyone. I don't mix politics and art. Leave me alone."

My grandfather turned to the man on the floor. His eyes softened a bit; his university days came flooding back once more; it was as if history ceased its relentless charge ahead and stood at rest a moment. He could feel a kind of pressure behind each bleat of the frogs through the man's door. Briefly his heart seemed to skip a full beat to synchronize with the rhythmic sound.

"Then let me hear a poem of yours," my grandfather said.

Algis rolled back a little to rest on both elbows again, and for an instant my grandfather saw a glimmer of defiance in the man's eyes; meanwhile, Liudvikas seemed anxious.

"Poetry?" Liudvika snarled. "What's that prove?"

"I want to hear a poem," my grandfather insisted.

Algis rose to his knees, made two circles with his thumb at the spot Liudvikas had butted him with the barrel of the Sturmgewehr, and began slowly, reluctantly.

Only the third moon feels
its unnamable splotch in night skies,
stands aching between quarter and half…

When the Sturmgewehr fired, my grandfather watched the man on his knees clutch his chest, fold like a 'Z,' then topple back like an "N," knees up, shoulders pinned against the base of the bookcase, arms resting perpendicular to shelves. Two brass casings ejected from the rifle in a shallow arc, then struck the plank floor with a dull ring. Gun smoke gathered in a plume above the dead man's bookcase and lingered there. My grandfather looked to Liudvikas, speechless, while Liudvikas tucked the Sturmgewehr under one arm and snuffled a little from the gun smoke.

"What shit," Liudvikas said, nodding at the dead man. "You call that poetry?"

So this brings us to the moment your shadow appeared inside the door of Būsi Trečias.

I wiped sticky mead from my mouth, said, "You missed the Owner's story."

To which the Owner added, "Such is the fate of the Third One!"

Your shadow did not reply to either of us. Dark swirls blurred against the wall behind the Owner, a scarf unfurling from a neck.

"But you've probably heard hundreds of stories like the Owner's," I added. "The old days. The Ice Age. Betrayal. Retribution."

You settled next to me at the bar. I helped you with your coat. Had there been a storm outside? Your coat was damp and a freshness of ozone clung to it. You'd not changed your green dress. The hem at your right side was crinkled and saliva-stained where the bright red flews of the black Shepherd slobbered there.

I raised my tankard to you. "Congratulations," I said. "You are indeed the Third One!"

"Perhaps *you* are the Third One," you said to me.

"But you were the third to arrive," I replied.

"I realize that 'third' suggests an order of appearance," you said, "but it may also mean an equal portion of a whole that has three parts. How do know you are not simply the 'Third One' of three parts? And if that is so, then can you not see that you are necessary to complete the whole. Can you not see why you must stay in Lithuania?"

Your last few words seemed to brighten the Owner. He seemed to take great satisfaction that he could participate in the ending of my story, while I could not in his. He removed his elbows from the bar, tried to shape his red stubble to a point with both hands.

"So, mister," the Owner smirked, "will you stay or go?"

"He says he won't stay with us in Lithuania," you told the Owner, then turned to me as if I was expected to defend myself.

The Owner looked me up and down.

"Why do you want *him*?" the Owner asked you. "Why is *he* so special, anyway?"

"He is a poet," you replied, at which point the Owner glanced at me, wide-eyed.

Did you see his look? Or were you too enamored of your own strategic coercion?

"Well," the Owner said with a menacing smile, "in that case let's hear a poem!"

Had you any idea the terror the words of such a request now assumed? It was as if you knew the Owner's story of the slain poet of Spalviškiai.

"No," I replied and crawled back into my tankard, the image of the Owner's gloating face lingering with the inebrious sweetness of mead on my tongue. "Let's leave," I said to you. "I'll take my chances in your Fiat."

"And die stupidly?" the Owner said, smiled, and folded his arms over his chest, his jaw, mandibular, set square like a granite ledge.

The Owner filled a third tankard with mead. You took it from him, lost your face in the tankard. I must say I missed your face that moment, knew I would miss you more than I'd ever expected. Then the Owner took a first-rate pull on his tankard, sighed, and wiped his red beard with the back of a hand.

"I want to hear a poem!" he demanded.

"No!" I hissed, then he reached for the vile hand bell, shook it—and at once I seized his hand and his two eyes, one a shade of deep blue, deepest I'd ever seen, fathomless like history; the other steel, a kind of metal, implacable, stricken into our present. "And you're not ringing that fucking bell!"

I felt the Owner's wrist resist, not with fear, but with anger.

"Stop it!" you said to us both, face swirling with fear and confusion. "I'm sorry I brought it up."

When the Owner's wrist relaxed, I let it go. He nudged the hand bell aside, took up the bottle of mead, and topped your tankard. You quickly raised it to your lips and drank it down, deep—by one third, I swear—as if to somehow forestall another of the Owner's demands. But when I sensed the neck of the Owner's portentous bottle again near my own, his hand once more on the horrid cracked bell, you suddenly gathered your coat, clutched it under an arm, and fled the tavern.

I followed you outside to Totorių gatvė, hearing the Owner laughing and the muffled peal of the horrid cracked bell through the tavern door.

No one else was on the street as we made our way east. We passed two red flags, an entry to the courtyard of the Vilnius Disinfection Station. When I lagged a little, your shadow tilted left onto Liejyklos. I followed the distant shots of your heels on the brick of Daukanto aikštė. You dragged your coat on. You walked fast, as recklessly as you drove! When I caught you, you stood in the glare of a new streetlamp looming above dew-slicked pavement of the parking lot, behind which the Old Presidential Palace loomed. When I joined you in the conical patch of light, you raised your coat collar to the night breeze.

"I'll think about staying," I said, out of breath. "I'll let you know tomorrow."

"What are you so afraid of?" you asked. "Lithuania?"

"Poetry," I sniggered.

You laughed.

"And what will you know tomorrow that you do not know now?"

And there we were. Two in light. Darkness beyond the light. Behind that, the yellow pastel façade of the Palace, behind that a space of memories—the old clangor of bishops, tsars, hangmen, commissars, children dancing—and beyond that, only silence, and the dead.

"Tomorrow," I insisted.

You smiled, smoothed your forest-green skirt over the stain of the Shepherd, took my arm, and tugged me out the safety of light, off, deeper into the umbra of Old Town.

"Alright," you said, "but between now and tomorrow we've still a long, long night."

Tongues

I glanced left, then right, each way saw Aušrine's tumid, amber-bejeweled hands on my shoulders. She pressed hard. And though I could scarcely bear the vaporous five-star Metaxa on her breath, her albino-white hair, I faced squarely her half-shut eyes:

"Kalbėk su manimi," she said.

"I'll speak with you," I replied, "but use English, like I taught you." She gripped me harder. "And please remove your hands from me."

"All right," she put her tongue out, "but not until you tell me," she hiccupped, laughed without a grin, smile, anything—amazing. She could laugh without so much as a smirk. "Where are you going?" She slurred every word, even slurred the expression on her face.

"None of your business," I said.

"Oh, Mr. Big Shot American," she gurgled her words, then slipped back into Lithuanian, "Ar tai tavo nuomanė?"

"Yes," I replied, "I'm speaking for myself."

She stumbled backward a half step, her hands still fast to the tops of my shoulders. The force jerked me forward by similar measure—I hoped, then, to spring back a bit in the opposite direction and free myself from her bear paws.

But she still had me.

"What's the matter with you?" I said, annoyed as much by her actions as by her habit of asking me if I spoke for myself. Then I lowered my voice. I wanted to show her I was truly concerned. I was surprised that I could still speak so tenderly in her presence. "Aušrine, what is it?"

"Nothing," she groaned and swayed a little right, pressing my left shoulder downward, a fortunate motion, since then I was able to wriggle one shoulder free of her grip.

But she still had me by the other.

So I reached over, pried her other hand free.

She toppled, her back to me, turning as she spiraled down to her knees, rump in air, the slip of her skirt caught on the stiletto of one red pump, ripping the silk of the hem into a frayed vee.

I winced. Then winced again when I said, "Are you all right?"

I couldn't bring myself to say anything else. Poor devil. Signs were not right with her. And what had things come to when a man like me felt sorry for a woman like her? Only two years before, just after Liberation, when the Reds on their way out had gone balking and bashing things, I'd known her differently. Then she was a devil in full bloom—the sort I'd seen, recognized, tried mightily to resist, and even in my darker parts somehow championed! She was beautiful then, confident, went many nights knocking on doors on the floor of the bendrabutis where she lived and I lived in the Baltupio District of Vilnius. When one of her victims opened the door, she produced a bottle of Gloria, three-star Lithuanian konjakas.

"Hello," she said, grinning ear to ear. Her yellow teeth gleamed in the dim light of candles she'd placed in the hall, a routine, citywide blackout. "Let's drink to Liberation! Let's be friends!"

In those days, how could anyone have resisted her? Her three stars? How it felt to be unoccupied after fifty years? Spirits were high and seemed they'd stay that way forever. Soon she had several of my neighbors in the hall, all men, sloshed on her Gloria, sitting on floors against peeled paint, all making ridiculous grunting sounds. Every so often someone broke into a monotonous chorus of "Lietuva Brangi." 'Dear Lithuania. . . . Let your sons draw strength from the past!' I felt my back slip down the cool cement wall, my eyesight going, flickering, my final memory seeing her bent slightly over me, a vision. Her hair was reddish then and fell into my face. She stood sturdy, straight, triumphant, pouring more of her amber temptation for me, me with my hand stuck out like a supplicant, a sick unweaned calf. Gloria! Hallelujah!

I suckled at the konjakas.

"Are you all right?" she laughed with expressionless glee.

That was the last I recalled, was how I learned about her kind of devil. One who pretends to be your friend without touching a drop of Gloria herself! One who offers up the spirits of the ancients unchained, worse than Bacchus. One who manufactures desires in others without feeling them first in herself. And worse. Rumors were that she'd been a Party member in the Ice Age. It was plain to see. In those days just after Liberation she had vexed me!

But she was different now. She was on her hands and knees straight in front of me. I stared at her derrière. Not bad for a devil. Her lavender dress stretched tightly over her rear, shapely, like an apple, round about the hips and stem of the tailbone, a couple charming little bumps on the blossom end. A bit swollen. Old. All devils seemed outwardly old. Then her knees began to give. Her derrière swayed right. A heel of her shoe still poked through the gaping tear in the hem of her slip. She fell on her side, curling up like a boiled shrimp. I could hardly bear how I pitied her then. Why should I pity her? I despised the impulse to pity in myself and guarded against it in others. Yet, there she was, coiled, pickled in Gloria. I struggled with the impulse to rush forward, what rose in me like a great lump of conscience, and in fact after a little delay, stage of grace, rushed forward, and with a finger cleared a few weedy strands of white, peroxide-rich hair from her face. I tried to gaff her in the pits of her arms with my hands and winch her to her feet. She felt like an enormous puppet, gangling, inanimate, ready to receive and imitate any motion I transmitted to her body.

"I thought you didn't drink?" I asked my marionette.

I wriggled her arms, flailed them about in air, until her eyelids rolled half open. At last, she groaned, "Dievo!"

"Speak English," I grumbled.

God!"

But then she was speaking Lithuanian again, after I'd done so much to teach her English. Her using Lithuanian was disappointing. But was it my fault? She wanted to learn English, so I taught her.

I walked my devil-puppet to my old Soviet state bed, sat her there so she slouched against the wall near the headboard, then propped her upper torso with chicken-feather pillows either side of her so she wouldn't topple sideways.

She mumbled, "But it was you. My devil-may-care American tutor, who gave me this forked tongue," then chanted, "Le-la le-la le-la." Once she opened her eyes, didn't budge, spoke—

"I want my English lesson now."

"I'm glad you want to practice, but you're drunk!"

She waited. I crossed my arms.

"No," I went on. "You're in no condition."

"Yes, I am. Listen . . ."

Her tongue wagged automatically,

Everybody knows I love my toes.
Everybody knows I love my toes.
I love my nails, my knees,
my neck, and my nose,
but everybody knows I love my toes . . .

Come to the party.
Don't be late.
Eat all you want,
but don't eat the plate . . .

Miss Polly had a dolly
who was sick sick sick.
She called for the doctor
To come quick quick quick . . .

Then she shut her eyes, her forehead furrowed with pain.

I fetched my shower towel, wetted it, and rang it out over her, watched the water trickle onto her head, split into rivulets that wound their ways around her black roots and down her forehead, behind her large ears. I wiped her hands and arms with the towel. After a few moments she came to and, without a sound, flung the pillows away, bolted upright in my state bed, glanced a second or two at errant feathers she'd sent floating about my flat. She got up and staggered out my front door.

I was glad she was gone, but after a short while realized she'd infected me with a curiosity. What the devil was the matter with her? But at what cost could I ever find out? I was determined not to be caught up in her spiraling descent, if indeed it could be conceived of as descent, wherever her dizzying zigzagging path might lead. I left the door to my flat a little ajar, the way she'd left it, and listened, heard the lift motor whine, clunk to a stop, then jolt, descending again, or was it rising? I suddenly rose to push the door to my flat shut when I realized she may have changed her mind and sent the lift upward. Then I didn't hear anything at all. I ventured out of my flat and from the window at the end of the hallway watched her below, outside the bendrabutis, halting, stumbling, reaching up to clear a strand of white hair from her face, only to catch the sides of her face and cheeks with her sweating palms and smear her makeup into a kind of ridiculous black and red mask. She stumbled one last time. Her stiletto again caught the tear in the hem of her dress. Then she disappeared.

I was pretty sure I'd never see Aušrine again, and when I realized this, I suddenly knew I needed to see her, not out of affection, but to save her. I was sure I'd schooled her well in English, but it seemed so useless if the devil destroyed herself. The plain irony of her addiction to alcohol was too, too simple. A devil done in by her own deviltry. All my English done in by her stubborn self-destruction. Perhaps it had all started years after Liberation when she moved to an upscale flat on Šeškinės gatvė, bought with all her savings from the Soviet years, very pretty printed paper on the interior walls, orchids and lavender, honeysuckle vines, creamy white and sweet smelling, clinging and coiling up the fine red brick exterior. But how? There, her parties grew more opulent, what seemed cauldrons of konjakas, volumes of pork and beef, huge cepelinai, enormous bowls of barščiai and rūgštynė, beer and black bread, and giant cheeses seeded through and through with anise.

Aušrine carried heaps of food and drink in mountains atop platters, over her head, swinging them side to side, spinning among the celebrants in her flat, catching now and again an errant bit of food toppling over the side with her free hand and tossing it back on top.

"Eat," she said to me, looking down from beneath the porch of her serving platter. "You need to build your strength for this new Lithuania!"

She must have felt powerful living on Šeškinės. Why else would she have asked me, in halting English, to give her my American tongue? But just now, in my flat, gripping me in her bear paws, I could see that her hips were obviously distended from overeating, cheeks ballooning, calves swollen with water and weight gain. And, seeing her that way, so obviously fallen, other matters came into focus, things that had happened years before: the young Lithuanian women she'd fixed me up with, for which I told her I'd be eternally grateful; and another incident, the night Aušrine'd laid one hand on my shoulder then reached back with the other and delicately scratched the small of my back with the nail of her middle finger,

"Come on," she whispered.

Back then I'd understood her scratch to be straight-forward temptation. But now? The way she pawed me in my room? Going on and on in Lithuanian, drunk, demanding her English lesson? I sat upright in bed, and a small nervous impulse ran down my spine, remembering her nail, scratching there, wanting somehow for my thoughts to drain out of my head and into my stomach, legs, feet, anywhere they'd not annoy me so much. But they didn't, wouldn't. There was more. She'd lost her laugh lines, some from the konjakas, the way it slackened and elongated her face, and some from her increasingly serious outlook on things. Even while the Soviets had occupied the country, while she was a Party member, though a mere clerk at the Communication Center in Vilnius, she'd said, "Pain is good. Death must be better."

Then she could laugh at this expression. But her jokes were over now, and those laugh lines she'd lost had become different sorts of lines. She puttied them up with cosmetics from America, and she no longer laughed when she spoke about these new lines.

"The trenches," she called them, then doused her slightly bulbous, fire-red nose into a huge snifter of Gloria, and that was it. No humorous self-repartee, such as, "Those? My Maginot lines." She lost all humor, whether black, allegorical, ironic, self-deprecating, or morbid. She grew serious and hard and unbecoming the devil I'd known her to be. I missed her bygone humor as much as having to keep my guard up when she'd begin her devilment:

"Come on, just one more won't kill you."

or—

"Who will know? I know I won't tell."

or—

"What the hell. Life's too short. Isn't that what you say in America?"

And God help me if I'd say, "No," and "A thousand times no!" She'd come right back with her dolorous retort:

"I like a man who speaks plainly, but is that really you speaking? Or are these someone else's words?"

I knew I would never see her again if I left it up to her. And though I knew myself the sickness of my nostalgia for her bygone deviltry, knowing full-well the foolishness of reacquainting myself with her sort of person, I nevertheless, in spite of myself, in spite of all reason, resolved to ring her up, to see if there was anything, anything at all I could do.

I found her new address and phone number by first ringing an acquaintance, Birutė, who'd known her when we'd all three lived in the Baltupio District.

"You want to call Aušrine, that *devil?*" Birutė said. "Are you sure? . . . Well, all right, she lives in Kaunas now. When you see her tell her something for me. No, forget it, just don't tell her who gave you her number."

I phoned the number Birutė'd given me but no one picked up, something I'd always hated, a bit like praying and getting no answer. I wasn't responsible for that kind of silence. And this almost stopped me from contacting Aušrine altogether. Still, overcome by the idea that an earnest man may do some good, even on behalf of a devil, I caught the express train and an hour later stood on Lenin Prospect (or what had been that sort of "prospect" in Soviet times), heading for Aušrine's place, the Viešbutis 'Baltija.'

When I approached the 'Baltija,' I was heartened to see a Ford dealership adjacent. It was late, and the security lights glaring off the metallic automobile paints—deep greens, glossy blacks, and glittering purples—gave me a sickening sense of homesickness for America I'd been trying to shake for years. Despite Aušrine's obvious addiction to Gloria, and seeing such a glittering example of the new entrepreneurship in her country, I had hopes that Aušrine'd found a nice place to live in Kaunas. She'd wanted to learn English to start a translation business. In the new Lithuania, the Lithuania of NATO and the European Union, there was no end to the need for translators. But all my hopes for Aušrine's material success vanished when I entered the lobby of the 'Baltija,' a decrepit mausoleum of Soviet architecture. The lift wires knocked about inside the shaft as I ascended to the fifth floor. The horrid basil-colored hall carpets smelled of rancid vodka—and God only knew what other substances contained in human vomit. The locks on most doors were broken off. Holes the doorframes where latches fit had been patched over with thin, cheap pine slats, and new locks screwed in off-center, so entire locks could be easily pried out—and had been. All the lights in the hallway had been bashed out. No earnest thief would be denied access. Nor would I.

I made my way to the farthest end of the darkest hall, guided only by the pale light of a third-moon that shone feebly through a window at the end of the hall. The moon was lying on its back, close to the horizon, its crescent full with a spleenish yellow-green. I felt for the raised iron numbers over the doors at the tops of the frames until I felt '318,' then knocked.

I tossed a little speech about in my head, in Lithuanian and English. If she dared come to the door in a place like this I'd have to convince her I was who I was before she'd let me in. I heard the lock turn twice, the door scrape against the frame, and at last open. She stood in her night coat, open in front, pale blue lines of her bra and slip showing through. She held her head with her palms on either side of her face, hung over, I supposed. Then she ran her fingers from the sides of her face back, through her hair, where it seemed to rustle and snap with electricity while particles of lint and a feather from her pillow floated about her person, all given an eerie blue shade by third-moon light.

She opened her eyes and grumbled a little, then grunted just once and went back into her room, leaving the door open. I entered, closed the door, and double locked it. She sat on a lumpy, broken-backed state bed, on a ratty spread printed vaguely with odd, primitive figures resembling a herd of wild boars. The air was damp and cool in the room, coming in through a window propped open with a stick smeared halfway up the stem with dried, dark red paint. Beyond the window stood a dead tree, divided in its middle so that the remaining branches looked like fingers of two hands positioned somewhere between begging and praying. The tree was backlit by a purplish light coming from a lamp hung over the door of an old bakery, though the air in the room smelled nothing like a bakery at all, more of rotted olives. The lamp snapped and sparked as insects disintegrated in bright flashes.

Aušrine crossed her legs, so the night coat fell away and exposed a sliver of her thigh, riven with several long stretch marks. One sandal hung by the big toe of one foot and she imparted just enough energy that it swung back and forth in the air slightly, keeping time. I watched the odd ticking of her sandal and, at last realizing she had not spoken at all, started to speak myself, to say what I'd come to say, thinking that when she didn't reply I'd leave and that would be that.

"I came to see if you were all right," I said.

She pointed her long nose in my direction.

"Me? Look at you. Calling at this hour."

"Okay, then," I began to mumble. My body wobbled a little and the soles of my shoes seemed to go weak. "What I mean is, you don't seem yourself. You don't seem normal. The old you, you know? You're headed for some kind of trouble. I mean, if there's anything I can do. If you need someone to talk to."

Then she started all over again, "Le-la le-la le-la le-la," hurling the sounds at me, now with even more passion and a grim smile on her face, on and on, "Le-la! le-la!"

She kept repeating her gibberish, and it was at last too much. I reached down, placed my hand over her mouth. I pressed hard. She rose from the bed, and by the time I knew she had me, first by both shoulders, and then with that familiar scratching along my spine with the edge of one, pointed nail. My soul shivered, and I removed my hand from her mouth.

"Dievo!" she gasped.

"English!" I said, with venom. "English!" I pleaded. "Can't you see I want to help? Don't you see why I'm here?"

When she pressed her mouth to mine, parted my lips with hers, I put my tongue in her, yet felt hers slide along the buttoned edge of my own, deep, deeper, until her tongue seemed to split, coil about, and imprison my own at its thick, red root. Then she pulled her tongue out.

While I remained mute, she whispered, smiling as she had in the impassioned days of liberation. "I know why you have come," she said in perfect English. "It simply goes without saying." She crossed the room to the window. The purple light continued to hum and fingers of the divided tree to beg and pray. "You poor thing."

Biography of a Gallstone

Dainava, wife of the famed man and his wondrous gallstone, the inter-
preter, and the American stood in Dainava's kitchen, what had been in
the old days a stall in the carriage house of the old Tiškevičiai manor.
Dainava wrung her hands as she spoke in Lithuanian, her eyes dead on the
American, while the interpreter, on tiptoes, spoke English straight into the
American's right ear. The old wife of Darius had a long, gray, glum face
that every now and again wrinkled into a grin, accentuated by the glint of
three gold teeth appearing out the right side of her mouth, which would
vanish and reappear as her facial expressions assisted her in delivering her
story.

According to Dainava, where the miraculous gallstone grew was without
doubt, not in the clean and lustrously lit annals of history, but darkly, in
a pear-shaped sac under the right lobe of her husband's liver. The man
destined to produce the wondrous stone lived in Vilkaviškis, a city whose
origins, like the history of the great stone itself, are accounted for by
various legends. But Dainava went on to say that, even with the forces of
luminous myth behind the amazing gallstone, history, that *bitch* ("wolf"
or "dog" she managed to add, "with perfect, painful teeth"), had scarcely
noticed its dark, apocalyptic coming, except for the American, who'd come
far for the sole purpose of viewing it.

Yes, she told her visitors, the world had all but forgotten Darius's
achievement. Vilkaviškis was a town with other worries, had been the loca-
tion of the German-Russian Front in the Second World War (or Russian-
German Front, depending on whom one asked), and had been completely
destroyed except for the sewing factory and two other buildings locals now
cannot identify, not including the bažnyčia, whose two steeples had been
blown off and insides gutted by bombers. Its holy walls remained awhile,
until the Soviet occupation of 1945, at which time the sandstones of the
bažnyčia gradually disappeared only to reappear little by little with the
raising of the Communist Cultural Center across the street.

So much history, so much going on, how could Darius, of all people,
have guessed the miraculous stone was growing in him? He knew nothing
of his delicate condition, the pathological concretion of cholesterol crystals
sprouting out an ulcer in his bile sac, which doctors now surmise was the
result of some monstrous and unnatural aggravation of bile and tissues.
No one could possibly have imagined the stone would grow to its miracu-
lous size, some nine years in the making, medical professionals guessed,
the girth and proportion Darius's wife, Dainava, would later compare to
that of a guinea pig, and its color to the immaculate alabaster of the sand-

stone bricks of the bažnyčia that had vanished in the Soviet occupation.

Initially, what had escaped Dainava, so she told the American and his interpreter, was precisely the miraculous nature of the stone that had grown inside of her husband. She had always known her husband to be special, felt he was destined for something extraordinary. After all, Darius was likely the descendant of the legendary, alleged sixteenth-century founder of Vilkaviškis, one "Vilkaujiškis," the "wolf-man," who came out of the forests one day and appeared before the Birštonai lords and, solely by the powers of his storytelling, persuaded them to uproot their tribes from native soil and move to the lush, flat, wolf-inhabited lands between the Vilkaujos and Šeimenos rivers.

What faith! What daring! What a tale this Vilkaujiškis must have told them!

Dainava always believed that her Darius possessed his ancestor's gift of storytelling because Darius had, for instance, convinced most locals that over the years the wolves in the forests surrounding Vilkaviškis had died or, through a mysterious process of evolution, had become werewolves. He claimed that the werewolves kept company in the forest at a rally once a month (not at the full moon, but by appointment coinciding with Party meetings, and quite like them), where they would rub snouts, paw leaves, nip ears, and sniff one anothers' behinds.

Dainava believed with all her heart that, like his daring ancestor, Darius's special place in history would be confirmed once and for all by the famous Soviet surgeon in Kalingrad (whose name is lost to history) while Darius lay in a sedated stupor.

"No man," the famous surgeon said, "can possibly survive surgery to remove such a stone."

The Soviet surgeon's words were particularly bothersome to Dainava because he had already removed it!

So Darius had only to live to make the miracle—and that he did!—at which point the proud Soviet surgeon quickly proclaimed it the largest gallstone known to science, adding that no American could possibly produce such a stone—and survive its removal.

The hospital was simply abuzz with news of the gallstone. And one would have thought that all the astonishing medical discourse surrounding it would have made Darius also feel proud of his crystalline progeny, perhaps supply some kind of impetus for a sort of maternal imprinting between Darius and his stone, though, as fortunes go, his body mended but his mind did not. He could not fathom that such a monstrous thing had issued from him. He grew glum and silent. He set it on the breakfast table and stared at it, and as each moment of silence passed, so did the luster of his storytelling. It was as if all his imagination had crystallized, been removed from him, and rested next to his plate of fried eggs and herring. Eventually, he could not bear to look at the stone at all. Worse than this, his coworkers at the pea-canning factory pestered him constantly to bring it to work and show it to them, to let them touch it and to lay their fingers along his scar, nearly a half-meter long and having never healed in the usual sense: the incision and places the stitches had gone through looked like two rows of ghastly violets in perpetual bloom along a ruby-red irrigation ditch.

Some blamed Darius's depression on the stone, others on the pressures of everyday life, of pea-canning,. Still others blamed the embarrassment such city-wide acclaim had laid at his doorstep. Upon seeing the stone or his ghastly scar, some people began to drop rubles into his palms, and it soon became clear to him that his co-workers at the pea-cannery and friends must have believed he was not normal, a freak, could no longer fit in among them, and in his mind the stone and the strangeness of his new income were a sign that he'd become bourgeoisie.

When his wife Dainava convinced him to donate the miraculous stone for the glass display case in the old Tiškevičiai manor house (famed for its occupation in 1812 by Napoleon and his quarter-million French troops or so, and for being the place from which Napoleon had declared war on Russia), Darius went utterly mad, believed this was an unmistakable sign that he was in fact bourgeoisie (not to mention the French origins of the word itself!). He went down to the basement of the converted Tiškevičiai carriage house where he and Dainava lived and attempted to hang himself by the robe-strings of a rotund, red-faced priest who'd left them hanging by a nail near the coal chute years before, along with a rosary, to commemorate his four years of hiding in the basement when Stalinites closed the seminary in town and began yet another round of deportations to Siberia.

But, as Dainava explained to the American and his interpreter, Darius failed in his suicide attempt, owing to her quick action. When below her very feet she'd heard Darius yelp and growl, wolfishly of course, she rushed downstairs with a kitchen knife to confront whatever sort of beast had gotten into the basement. Instead she found her Darius swinging from a beam. Holding the knife high over her head, she rushed to him and, hesitating only a moment, since, after all, he was swinging by his neck by holy robe-strings, and commemorative ones at that, she summarily sliced them in two, at which point he fell to the dirt floor, doubled over. Dainava quickly took the rosary off the nail nearby and began giving him last rites, until he began rasping for air, then shot straight up, stumbled up the stairs, fled Vilkaviškis, and never returned.

So accustomed to her own surroundings at the converted carriage house of the Tiškevičiai manor where she had lived her whole life, and so taken with her own narrative of the miraculous stone and her hapless Darius, Dainava scarcely noticed how anxious and impatient the American's interpreter had become. The interpreter had assumed to *see* the miraculous stone, presumably because her American employer had hired her to accompany him to Vilkaviškis to make inquiries about purchasing it. And to top it all, the American was very tall, owing to his Texas heritage (so he said of himself), and the interpreter found she had to repeatedly go on tiptoes to get the words into his ear over Dainava's vigorous narrative—and now her toes hurt, which reminded her of the runways of Paris and her failed modeling career which she blamed in part on Nature (she was too short), in part on her mother (who'd sent her to France looking like Jackie Onassis, at least forty years out of date), and in part on the Soviet Union for not crumbling two years earlier when she was in her prime—nineteen). She also blamed her failure as a Parisian model on a small scar in the middle of her forehead, about the size of a pea. But at the very moment Dainava might have noticed the interpreter's discomfort, the American launched into his own narrative, aided by the interpreter, of course. He seemed inspired somehow by Dainava's rousing story of the glorious stone, and seemed determined to tell his own amazing story, as Americans were famed to do. He combed back the handlebars of his blazing red moustache, stuck his hands into the deep pockets of his cardigan sweater, and said how a vicious looking dog had stopped his bus coming into Vilkaviškis. The animal had stood squarely in front of the bus in the center of route A-7 from Marijampolė, squatted in the shape of a large question mark, and shat precisely on the centerline of the highway.

("'Shat?'" the interpreter asked the American. "Do you want me to interpret 'shat' for this old woman?"

"Yes," he replied. "'Shat.' Do I have the correct form of the verb?")

The American then went on to say the most curious thing was the defecating dog's smug sense of invulnerability to the bus, no fear, nothing, just a passing look as it finished dropping its load, straightened itself momentarily into the shape of a hyphen, then trotted off the highway!

"Could this creature have been the 'wolf' imbedded in the town's name and history?" the American asked. "Could that have made it so smug?"

(The interpreter, who had been with the American on the bus over from Vilnius, replied without consulting or interpreting for Dainava.

"It's ridiculous for you to think so. All the wolves are gone from Vilkaviškis. Only the name remains—and a dim history. That was just an ordinary dog shitting in the road."

"But to have shat—'shat,' is that right?" the American said, "precisely in the center of the road is surely extraordinary for an ordinary dog.")

Then Dainava, who'd been pretending to follow the exchange between the American and the interpreter, though she knew not a word of English, reached into her large apron pocket, removed the miraculous stone itself, the very one, and plunked it into the interpreter's hand, fully filling her palm, who instantly handed it to the American and tucked her hands in the back pockets of her outdated black market Levis. Then, without looking at either Dainava or her American employer, the interpreter broke into her own story, twice-told of course, in Lithuanian and English, saying that as a child she had lived in the very same carriage house in which they all now stood, at which time Dainava wiped a great glossy tear that threatened to drip out her right eye, hugged the interpreter, then stepped back and clamped the interpreter's face between her two hands and kissed her on her forehead.

"And I remember your mother, Rita! Oh my," she added, "what have you done with your hair?" (For the interpreter had not forsaken the Jackie-O look since Paris).

It turns out that Rita and her family had lived in the carriage house in the old days, too, and Dainava went on to say how Rita (rest her soul) had been a good Party member and worked hard at the sewing factory many years and devoted her life to the Soviet cause, though Dainava regretted that Rita had never been promoted to the pea-canning plant—as Dainava herself had—which, Dainava explained, was probably for the best, since after being promoted to the pea-cannery herself the whole operation had been corrupted by workers stealing peas meant for the Party store and Party officials, when in reality all these crooked pea-cannery employees might have gotten perfectly good peas if they regularly attended Party demonstrations.

The interpreter replied that as a child she'd heard the story of the stolen peas and remembered it all too well, but that she did not remember her mother, Rita, or her early childhood, say, before age nine.

"Nothing before age nine?" the American asked, amazed.

"Well, not exactly nothing," she replied. She went on to explain that, while living at the carriage house with twenty-two other families, she and her sister had run with a pack of twenty or so other children, wild, day and night, because most parents of children at the carriage house had been good Party members. Both mothers and fathers spent many days at the factories and nights at Party meetings. In fact, she went on, she had no recollection of herself as herself until one day when the pack of children she ran with divided itself into two groups and declared war on one another. The matters on which the division occurred she could not recall, only that her older sister was general of one group and one day simply declared war on the other group by throwing stones at them. Things, she explained, escalated, until all the children of the carriage house were at war with one another over this or that while their parents were off building the Soviet future.

One day during a particularly vicious skirmish, she herself was knocked unconscious by a blow to her forehead from an unusually large stone. She woke a full five minutes later, so they told her, and suddenly realized that she was, well, herself, and this moment was the beginning of all her personal recollections. She also supposed that her near-death experience was the cause of her unnatural adolescence—marked by the pea-sized pockmark on her forehead. At this point in her story the interpreter turned away from Dainava and to the American and began speaking to him solely in English. She was sure, she said, that the stone's blow to her noggin had been responsible for her perilous behavior in Soviet times—smuggling Beatles and Zappa and Zeppelin tapes and all sorts of Party-banned books through Kalingrad. When the first television arrived at the carriage house, she remembered gathering with other like mal-affected teens (most of whom claimed they had been similarly stricken by stones on their foreheads) around it to watch Brezhnev make his speeches and giggling and joking in whispers about how they would have to lie the next day at school, would have to say these were important and wonderful speeches, how they would not believe their own lies, and how they spoke only in whispers because they were sure one family who lived upstairs in the carriage house was KGB.

The interpreter's mother, Rita, had once caught her with contraband, containing, as she recalled, "Helter Skelter," and immediately whisked her away to the "Mažučių Šaltinėlis," the "Magic Stream," where she forced the interpreter's head beneath the icy clear water for its all-purpose healing powers. Pagans, Christians, and atheists alike used the water. Pagans believed the stream emanated from some primeval source deep in the earth and full of cosmic energies; Christians revered the day a little girl from town swore she saw the Virgin Mother washing her hair in the stream; and atheists had gone to the trouble of having the water analyzed and proclaimed it a bounteous broth of medicinal salts. What a watering hole for animals of all stripes! But when Rita removed the head of her mal-affected offspring from the wondrous stream, it had little effect. Even the tragedy of one of the teachers at her school did not dissuade her from her devious behavior. The teacher at the Vilkaviškis school had lost his job because someone heard him make a joke about Brezhnev and then they found out he'd attended a secret church service. The teacher had five children and a wife and was now the poorest of the poor. Since Liberation the only hope for the teacher's family to bring itself out of eternal poverty was the youngest son who had a talent for music, so they scraped together all their savings and sent him to Los Angeles to try to become a famous rock'n'roll star.

It was just about this time that Dainava, who'd not been getting any of the interpreter's personal story in Lithuanian language, but noticed a flicker of a smile on her, believed the interpreter had been speaking fondly of her Young Pioneer days. (What else could she have been so enthusiastically speaking of?) Dainava looked at the interpreter with large puppy eyes, then proceeded to plead with her to model her daughter's Young Pioneer's uniform, just to make an old woman happy, just for old times' sake, at which time the interpreter, glancing desperately at the American and hoping he hadn't understood a word of the old woman's Lithuanian, asked Dainava why her own daughter couldn't model the nostalgic uniform for her.

"No, no," Dainava said, "can't you see how she is? Pregnant! And with two of her other children running wild about the carriage house—somewhere?"—but which Dainava quickly explained was not a problem since she had always fancied herself as a mother and could properly take care of any number of generations of children if only her daughter's husband weren't in prison and oh, oh, what would she do?

The interpreter glanced at Dainava.

The old woman's puppy eyes glowed.

"You're small," Dainava said to her, "it will fit you."

At last, the two women went away and then returned, Dainava beaming, her bulbous-bellied daughter standing in the back of the room of the carriage house scowling, her two absent children suddenly present and shrieking without mercy in the outer hall—and the interpreter in full Young Pioneer regalia, turning to Dainava and smiling, then turning to the American and whispering in viperish English.

"You will have to pay *extra* for this," she told her American employer.

Then the interpreter began translating Dainava's words as she began pointing out the features of the uniform to the American—

"Notice the pretty deep blue skirt . . .

"And the clean white blouse . . .

"And these smart brass buttons . . .

"Along with the official bars on the shoulders . . .

"And the red neckerchief, tied to make three points, each an aspect of the Communist credo . . . which is . . . was . . . well, there are three points . . . and here is the most important thing anyway . . ."

She gestured at a small pin on the lapel of the blouse, a five-pointed red star.

"You see?" she said. "My daughter was nearly ready to be promoted to Young Communist!" The old woman nodded in her scowling, pregnant daughter's direction. "Well, that was before her first child and, well, you know, look at her now." Dainava went on. "And look here, just inside one point of the red star in the lower right-hand corner. Do you see the portrait of Lenin as a child? Adorable, don't you think?" Then Dainava glanced at the interpreter. "Do you remember the Young Pioneer oath?"

The interpreter shot another piercing look at the American.

"No," she said to Dainava.

"Of course you do," Dainava said. "Come on, say it with me."

The two women started slowly:

"We Young Pioneers of the detachment bearing the name of . . . ("Well, let's just say 'Comrade Darius,'" Dainava interjected) . . . bearing the name of Comrade Darius solemnly swear to be faithful upholders of the great cause of Lenin, Stalin and the Great Revolution and to never betray secrets . . ."

Dainava's eyes began to swell then redden and all of a sudden she was overwhelmed with something like nostalgia and began wailing for her lost Darius.

"He's alive!" she said. "I know it!" And she went on to say she'd heard he'd been sent to Siberia but that now he was free and hiding somewhere. "He is afraid. He is mad. But he is a man with a miraculous gallstone, and I miss him!"

Dainava said she missed Darius desperately, missed him more and more each passing day, at which point the American used Dainava's moving ejaculations to plant the gallstone back in Dainava's hand, hoping it might give her some comfort. She took the stone and rolled it along one side of her face, saying the stone was all she had left and that someday either the miraculous stone or Darius or both would save her, saying that now she lived only on her old Communist Party pension which was nearly worthless these days, and now, soon, she would have no alternative but to go to the bažnyčia and beg the priest for charity. How humiliating! She looked for the interpreter (who'd fled the room to remove the Young Pioneer uniform) and then to the American and chattered on in Lithuanian into empty air until the interpreter reappeared and translated.

"She says she's humiliated because by going to the church to ask for charity she will have to break her sacred vow of atheism."

"I see," said the American. "You know, I don't think any country or church or whatever should force its beliefs on anyone no matter who they are or what they do or don't believe in or whatever their race or creed or color or—"

The interpreter interrupted him by stabbing her right arm straight out into the air.

"Stop!" she said. "How do you expect me to interpret that? What on earth are you talking about?"

. . . meanwhile, Dainava seemed to change. Her eyes began to clear and she dried them on her apron. She pitched the miraculous stone from hand to hand. Everything in the room of the converted carriage house became quiet. Even the shrieking children in the outer hall were quiet—or gone (wherever they could have gotten to) and it seemed that even the heavens themselves stood still in those moments when fate or predestination or something or other was at work.

Dainava licked her lower lip.

"Whether Darius is dead or alive, we must give this miraculous stone a future," she said. "It must have a place in this world. For Darius's sake. For my children and their children's sakes. For all our sakes! Follow me!"

Without removing her apron, without hesitation, Dainava went out the door, but not before finding the interpreter, interlocking her right arm with the interpreter's left, and towing her along. Only then did the interpreter notice she had not yet removed the Young Pioneer's blouse or Lenin's brooch pinned to it and let out a little gasp in horror that she was being towed into public. The American followed the two women and the little troop of three marched rapidly up Karosas gatvė, past the converted stables and its twelve families, to the brand new bažnyčia, its two copper-clad steeples shining in the afternoon sun, its immaculate alabaster walls the same color as the gallstone Dainava clenched in her fist.

Dainava paused at the entrance of the bažnyčia, trembled slightly, then leaned into the heavy door with all her weight and went straight inside. The three of them made good time along the nave until reaching the prayer rails lining the altar and hundreds of half-melted prayer candles. At this point Dainava became weak in her knees, seemed to half kneel, then she shot back up, stiff-straight, her gyrations nearly knocking the interpreter, who was still interlocked on her arm, off her feet.

Quite by chance a priest appeared from one wing of the bažnyčia and, seeing the three of them standing there, took himself back a half-step, then busied himself nervously with the altar, centering the chalice and covering it to protect it from dust, which was still plentiful in the aftermath of the feverish construction to get the bažnyčia ready as soon as possible after liberation from the Soviets. Dainava unlatched the interpreter, who then immediately reached up to her chest and secretively removed the brooch of Lenin, then ran back a few paces to stand with the American to interpret for him.

Dainava walked up to the altar and stood beneath the familiar statue of the crucified Christ. She thrust the gallstone in her hand out for the priest to see, and when she was sure she had his attention, said, "Father, my husband was a good man. He worked in the pea-canning factory. For years he grew this miraculous stone inside him. Nine years, the doctors said! It is certainly the largest and most miraculous stone ever removed from a man in either hemisphere. My husband, rest his soul, for I am sure he was mad and was deported, was martyred like, like, well, like so many priests, maybe like yourself. He gave his life so others can believe in miracles."

All the while Dainava had been speaking she was edging her way closer and closer to the altar, and when she was nearly there, she thrust the stone into one hand of the startled priest.

"Surely, your Holiness," she went on, "if anything these days is a holy relic, this is. Can't you use it? Put it on display? Charge people to touch it? You know, like in the old days? This stone was consecrated by the old mayor of Vilkaviškis and kept at the Tiškevičiai manor house! Well?"

"My child," the priest cleared his throat and set the stone on the altar, then quickly removed it and held it nervously. "Certainly, the Church was founded on a rock, but that doesn't mean that just any stone is holy. Take for instance the stone in Vištytis that is shaped like a devil's footprint. You know, I have heard that pagans used to perform sacrifices on it. Listen, if you need charity—"

"I don't want charity!" Dainava said. "I want to sell my husband's holy gallstone to you! This stone is not a rock I found by the road or the Devil's doing. It came out of my husband! Doesn't the church buy and sell these sorts of things anymore? Just last week 1,600 pilgrims from Poland came through town on their way to see the Miraculous Black Madonna of the Gates of Dawn in Vilnius. Surely some of them might pause to—"

"I am afraid not," he interrupted, "not *that* stone." The priest handed the stone back to her and laid a comforting hand on her shoulder and grew a warm grin on his face. "Perhaps," he added, "I will see you at our concert tonight. It's very special. The Choir of Political Prisoners and Deportees will be performing. There is no charge, of course."

Dainava began tapping her foot, first the left, then the right.

"So you're saying it's worthless?—all the anxiety that produced all the bile that produced this huge stone, all the suffering for all these years that went into this was all for nothing? Father, it was immaculately conceived! My Darius was a pure-hearted man. And he wasn't bourgeoisie. He wasn't!"

"Yes, my child," the priest said politely.

Dainava suddenly grew a shade of green on her face. She turned back to look at the interpreter and the American in the aisle, then forward to cast one last pleading look at the priest, then cocked her arm with the hand with the miraculous stone in it.

"Then, you can have it back!" she shouted. "For nothing!"

She hurled the gallstone straight at the crucified Christ, where it struck

Him square on the forehead, ricocheted off, then bounced off a prayer rail and flew straight into the American's hands, who, startled by his miraculous catch, juggled it a second or so as if it were a hot potato.

The interpreter, perhaps remembering her own life-altering blow to the forehead when she had been a child, reached up, and with a nearly religious reflex, touched the spot on her forehead where she'd been stricken years before, her pea-scar, half-believing that perhaps some sort of miracle might happen to her, that she might be blessed and bleeding there, when Dainava suddenly pointed at the crucified Christ and shouted, "Look, Father! It is a miracle! Jesus is bleeding out his forehead. Look! Blood! Real blood!"

The priest ran quickly and stood at the feet of Jesus and began examining the statue's forehead, cocking his head back and sideways at many painful angles to try to locate the miraculous blood that Dainava had said was dripping from Christ's forehead. But Dainava, satisfied that she'd made the priest pay, grew a twisted smile on her face, turned, marched rapidly back down the aisle, again towing the interpreter who towed the American, to the front door. Dainava opened the door, pushed both her companions through, then slammed it resonantly shut.

Later in the day the interpreter and the American took the bus back to Vilnius. From time to time the American shifted painfully in his seat. His knees were wedged against the seat in front of him. It would be a long ride and they would arrive very late, but the interpreter had wanted it that way, because, she said, it would not necessitate staying the evening in Vilkaviškis, a boring town, she said, because she knew, because it was her hometown, to which the American said, "Of course you think it's boring because you grew up there." (Upon hearing this the interpreter again touched that spot on her forehead where the stone had smacked her.)

And the American continued to disagree.

"I found Vilkaviškis fascinating," he said, then added, "you see?" as the bus swerved suddenly left to avoid hitting a hay wagon entering onto route A-1, then having overcompensated left, cut sharply right to miss a drunk staggering along the opposite berm.

The interpreter replied, "Perhaps so," and let her eyes fall to the deep blue skirt and red neckerchief she had folded neatly on her lap.

"And," the American said, his eyes following hers down to her lap, "Dainava was very kind to give you her daughter's Young Pioneer outfit, don't you think?"

A small groan escaped the interpreter's throat. Then she reached over to the American's stomach and patted a curious bulge that appeared to be growing under his cardigan sweater.

BIOGRAPHY OF A GALLSTONE

"Did you pay her much for your new baby?" she laughed. "Or should I call it your pet 'guinea pig?'"

"Yes," the American replied, "it cost me a pretty penny. But someone had to do it. I'm sure Darius's gallstone will have a place, a real future in America. After all, what a history!—and this stone just may be the most monstrous of its kind."

It was then that the bus slowed, the brakes whined, and it came to a dead stop on route A-7 just before leaving the city limits of Vilkaviškis. The interpreter and the American craned their necks forward . . .

"See!" the American told her excitedly. "I told you! That's no common dog! Look at it! Have you ever seen an ordinary dog shit in the road like that? Just like that? Twice in the same day? Right on the center line?"

Green Fire Ponds of Molėtai

The force that through the green fuse drives the flower Drives my green age . . .
-Dylan Thomas

Summer, and cows scatter over and pasturelands of Molėtai, Lithuania. Its sallow, rolling hills and thin, high clouds rush over parched earth, patching it with swift-moving shadows. When the wind stiffens, the American volunteer detects the scent of manure and notices in the distance three children milking a cow. One child stands at the head; another squats at the udder and fills the pail. One of the children is singing—but which one? The wind blubbers in the volunteer's ears, making it impossible to tell.

Mrs. Domarkienė, Principal of the agricultural school, leans on an old Soviet paršiukas, 'pig-snout bus.' She bends deeply at her knees and they crack, once, twice, then takes a handful of straw from the barnyard and casts it adrift in the breeze. It sails over the pastureland, scatters. She pinches the right hinge of her eyeglasses and draws them off her nose. Her thick-lensed spectacles cast a virescent glint in the sunlight.

"*Damn* hot," she says and turns to the American. "Have I said it correctly? *Damn?*"

"Yes." The volunteer winces and adds, "Those children?"

"Orphans," Mrs. Domarkienė says. "They live at the agricultural school and work at the farm."

The school's watchman joins them, limping, a head of dark hair and stubble bristling, running high on cheekbones, its burly rows interrupted by two scars, one in the shape of a partial moon at the right corner of his mouth, where he rubs it frequently, as if trying to wipe it off. The other scar, shaped like a bird with spread wings, hovers over his left eye, but he never seems to touch it.

The watchman squints at the volunteer, all the while tossing back red Anykščių wine from an amber bottle, rivulets of it pulsing down deep creases along his mouth and jaw. He staggers to the pig-snout, then unsteadily gets behind the wheel.

"I can drive," the volunteer whispers nervously to Mrs. Domarkienė. "After all, I'm here to work."

"Driving is the watchman's job," she says. "And you are not really a volunteer because of the *snafu*—have I said it correctly, *snafu?*'"

The volunteer seats himself alone in the rear of the pig-snout. Mrs. Domarkienė protests briefly—"Join us!"—but he falls silent, thinking of how Mr. Puškevičius in Chicago, or someone, had not notified the school he was coming.

Pig-snout lurches forward, nearly runs off the road. After the near-calamity, the watchman turns slightly to the rear to address the volunteer.

"It will snow today," he says.

"You mean it will *not* snow today," the volunteer tells the watchman. "It's summer."

"The watchman means it will snow today," Mrs. Domarkienė says, laughing.

The watchman goes on: "You American. I *life* you."

Mrs. Domarkienė leans to one side correct the watchman, but the volunteer interrupts her.

"You mean you *like* me," he says to the watchman.

"No." The watchman grins ear to ear under the bloom of his whiskers. "I *loff* you."

"You can't *love* me," he replies, hastily.

Mrs. Domarkienė slumps back, flat against her seat, rolls her eyes, and turns to stare out her window. Later she turns her head to one side, talks over the headrest, says to the volunteer, "The watchman loves you."

She chuckles and goes on to tell the watchman's story:

"Before being the watchman at our school, he was in the Red Army," she says. "He liked being in the army. It was his career. He was very proud. He was an intelligence officer. A captain. Head of a battalion. About forty men.

"They were ordered to go to the Soviet border with China, far into the mountains where it was very cold. And snows. The environment was so harsh in this region that many of his men were volunteers for the assignment. Maybe this is why he says he loves you. Because you are a volunteer.

"The watchman knows the Chinese language. He studied it in university. This is why he was the leader. He liked his men. He loved them. The watchman made jokes with his men. He told them he was their 'little czar.' They thought it was funny.

"One day, one of his men asked him, 'If you are a czar, then you can order the snow to stay away when we go on our mission tomorrow.'

The watchman told the man, 'All right, I command it: There will be no snow!'

Many of his men heard this and laughed.

"But on the intelligence mission the snow came. More snow than you can imagine. Everything was white. So much white it makes men invisible inside and out. They were lost. Hopeless. Three days. Half his men froze to death. Half the others lost hands, feet, or legs. The watchman lost all the toes on one foot."

They arrive at the school, a single story of pale yellow cinderblock. The watchman exits pig-snout, leans heavily on his good foot, looks all around himself, extends his arms and turns his palms up.

"What? No snow?" he says, grins, limps over to a fountain basin shaped like a donut, and sits on the rim above the dry pool. He leans far into the fountain basin, takes hold of a valve and twists it until water spits out the spigot. He remains on the rim of the fountain, removes his bottle of wine from a hip pocket, gulps from it, eyes rolling up as he drinks, pupils a deep shade of olive, sockets sunken, then shuts his eyes. His chin drops to his chest, and he sleeps.

That afternoon, the volunteer searches the school for Mrs. Domarkienė. When he approaches the lobby near the main entrance, she emerges from a water closet and sails toward him, her drably printed flower dress flowing about misty gray stockings that seem to press painfully into nets of blue veins. She pushes her glasses up the bridge of her nose, and accelerates, her steel heels ringing in the hallway. She seems tireless. Perhaps the only other sign that she is not superhuman in her administrative stamina and verve for the success of her agricultural school is a single lock of hair that constantly hangs in her eyes. Time to time she bats the lock with two fingers or blows at it with a puff of air from her lower lip, though always unsuccessfully, and so it ticks across the two windows of her industrious soul as if to remind one that time is passing, always.

"There must be more grain!" she says as she tacks past him and enters her office.

The volunteer stands outside her open door a short time. She invites him inside and explains that because the farm is no longer part of a Soviet collective, it struggles to make it as a for-profit dairy farm.

"We once had eighty cows; we now have eight," she says. "I am writing to Ministry officials for help."

She takes up a pen and begins to write, to puzzle out her problems on the page, upside down from where he stands and, of course, in Lithuanian language which he scarcely knows a word of. Her elbows stiffen with each thrust of her pen against the page, followed by a flurry of parries, trying to create the illusion of scientific optimism.

"I can help," the volunteer says, cheerfully. "I'm an agricultural engineer. It's my first time outside the States, but I'm ready to get to work."

She sets her pen precisely parallel to the long edge of her papers and leans forward. Her eyes meet his with an icy stare.

"Won't you please sit down?" she says.

Her green eyes meet his, the sort of green he imagines ignites life, courses and burns through stems of plants, through roots and into earth.

"I don't want to sit down," the volunteer says. "I want to work."

"Perhaps you would like to visit the old manor house across the street?

Inside is a beautiful collection of Second World War trophies found in our region—helmets, ammunition, sabers, Russian, German, Lithuanian partisan. And some objects from the Soviet years. In beautiful condition. Some are for sale."

"I don't want to visit the manor house. I didn't come here for souvenirs." By now the volunteer is aware that he is tapping his toe. He stops, says, "Can't you find anything for me to do?"

"Why do you want to work?" she asks.

"My wife has passed. I'm retired."

"I am widowed," Mrs. Domarkienė says, a wry smile growing on her face. He can almost see it grow doubly in the lower part of the lenses of her eyeglasses. "My husband perished in a Siberian prison. I will never be able to retire," she says, then adds, "and in America you begin to work when you retire?"

When she politely asks him to leave so she can finish her report, he pauses outside her door, hears pages flutter and the wooden, feverish scrawling of her pen.

That night the volunteer sleeps very little. He draws the bed sheets tightly between his knees like a tent, and when he begins to drowse, he keeps hearing a soft plop, plop onto the sheets. He rises, crosses the room, puts on the light, and sees several insects shaped like long black capsules of medicine emerge from nail holes in the wall by his bed, *juodasis* žygai her's heard, black wood beetles. They drop freely onto his bed and crawl off. He is horrified, goes down the hall to fetch the watchman, but finds him snoring inside his booth in a wine-induced stupor. He returns to his room, chews a couple sticks of gum, plugs the nail holes over his bed with it, and feels an absurd sense of accomplishment. In his final years, he has come to Lithuania from to volunteer, to donate his valuable time, to work! Now he plugs insect holes in walls. He's come all this way and all Mrs. Domarkienė can say is *I am sorry for the snafu*?

He flings open his window, feeds his lungs on the cool night air, his eyes on the quiet, silvery light of stars and bright full moon in the eastern sky. He muses, no wonder ancient peoples mapped the night sky long before its terrestrial counterpart. They had insomnia, too, staring endless hours at distant stars, not knowing that light they saw, cast millions of years before into the blackness of space, may have in fact died out. He felt like the light of a dead star. Perhaps he was useless ages ago and hadn't known it.

After a short time, in moonlight he spots the three orphans he'd seen that day in the pastureland—one girl and two boys. They walk hand-in-hand past the fountain, cross the road, and vanish into the trees surrounding the old manor house. The volunteer dresses quickly, exits the school, and follows them into the trees. He walks briskly along a narrow path, past several stagnant ponds dug to water cattle, now gone stagnant, musty, covered with algae that, in moonlight, glows green, seems to ignite ivy covering the ground, and spreads upward, burning everything around him.

When he comes to the manor house, its shadows are crisp and clear and its walls seem new and smooth in the silver light of the moon. He walks to the rear of the house and spies the three children standing in the center of an old playground, onto which the three children lead one of the cows. He reasons that earlier in the day they must have fetched the animal from the farm and concealed it in woods near the manor house.

One of the boys invites the other two to sit. Then he goes to the cow and places his hand on its forehead. He backs away a little and begins to sing in Lithuanian, a sorrowful and plainly felt song. Each child takes a turn, sings. Then all three sit on the silvery surface of the playground and say nothing to one another.

In the morning when he goes outside the school, the three orphans exit after him, rush past, and sit on the lip of the fountain. The waterspout now stands tall and glimmering, framed with mist of red, blue, green, and yellow light in prismatic brilliance. All three orphans are about thirteen years of age. All wear pants cutoff at the knees; black canvas sneakers with white rubber soles; and tee-shirts, though their tee-shirts are of different sorts. One is inscribed CALL OF DUTY, BLACK OPS; another, JUST DO IT; and the girl's, BABY ON BOARD. Only the girl's braless breasts budding beneath the cheap cotton fabric of her tee shirt distinguishes her from the boys.

The children dab sticks into the fountain, lift out wads of tannic-brown, waterlogged leaves, and fling them at one another. After a time each child glances at him, never two together, then all three head for the overgrown cinder running track, cross it, and walk in the direction of town. They cross the track walking. Only the girl still holds her stick. She pokes the rear-end of one of the boys, who jumps, swings around, and chases her through a high hedge at the far side of the abandoned running track.

The volunteer reenters the school and paces outside Mrs. Domarkienė's office. The pacing helps, but he is still angry and puzzled that he has come so far to work and there's nothing to do. Then he hears music coming from behind her office door, and at last he believes he has some excuse for opening it. He must seem to be curious. He'll ask about the music. He pushes her door inward and stands at the threshold awhile. Mrs. Domarkienė sits behind her desk with her glasses off and eyes closed. On the credenza behind her a record turns on a phonograph, an aria of some sort. She opens her eyes and quickly slips on her thick glasses without adjusting them. "It's from *The Magic Flute*," she says. "A recording by my only child. She lives in America now."

"She sings beautifully," he says.

"Yes," Mrs. Domarkienė replies, lowering her eyes, "more beautifully than any recording from America."

It is not Mrs. Domarkienė, it is the frail, beautiful sound of her daughter's voice from faraway America that sends him back to the manor house, alone. He crosses the road and follows a path mostly overcome with moss and creeping ivy. Now, in daylight, the algae-smothered ponds are dull green. And the drab hue reminds him he is without the work he imagined himself doing, his commitment to travel, to be of some use somewhere to someone. He remembers the green fire ponds the night before, wonders if their all-consuming glow, like his passion for work, had been merely an illusion.

In daylight, the three-story manor house is a pale rusty-colored brick, Doric columns pushing up the portico in a baroque manner, trimmed in a gray, moldy-colored white. He ascends the front stairs and tries the door, but it is padlocked. When he walks to the rear he finds the remains of the playground, loose mosaics of broken asphalt, some pieces elevated on tiny platforms by yellow, half-grown and dying tufts of weed that push up through the surface. He stands by the abandoned playground a long time. In the trees by one of the ponds a bird calls, yu, yu-yu-yu, yu, yu-yu. Here in the ruined playground the air is cooler, the light in the sky farther from him, quiet and silvery, and suspended in the west is the ghost of a full moon, drowned in daylight, a visage of uselessness. How feeble the afternoon moon!

From the manor house, he returns to the school, then sets out across the abandoned running track and down the main road. It is a beautiful lane. On both sides grow tall birches with brilliant white bark and leaves that quake in the hot breeze. Two silver-capped spires of the cathedral stand against the deep blue sky and mark the end of the lane.

Once in town he discovers a religious festival, enjoys the procession, the wagging hands of priests passing by, the brass incense pot swinging in its improbable, smoking arc through the air, and families singing songs for the blessing of rain. He doesn't go inside the cathedral for the service.

When he returns to the school he finds the three orphans sitting around the fountain, seeming pensive, gazing off in the direction of the festival. Mrs. Domarkienė steps out the main door of the school, a break from her writing. She slips her glasses off her nose, puts her hands on her hips, closes her eyes, and begins to stretch herself, forward, back, side to side. When she walks back inside the school he follows her and stops her before she enters her office.

He nods in the direction of the orphans outside.

"I would like to take them to the festival in town."

"No," she says, walks into her office, and closes the door.

"Why not?" he asks through her door loudly, impatiently.

Her voice carries back. "They have their work at the farm."

When the sun begins to set, he goes outside to stand near the fountain, its water spray nearly invisible in the gloaming, yet loud, echoic against the yellow cinderblock of the school, as if pleading to be seen. Inside his booth, the watchman wakes, comes out of the school carrying a paper sack, and sits on the rim of the fountain.

"Sit," the watchman says, but the volunteer nods, refuses.

A little later both of them watch Mrs. Domarkienė emerge from the school. Her steel heels ring wildly in the gloaming. She sits next to the watchman while the volunteer remains standing.

Mrs. Domarkienė says, "Won't you sit with us?"

But again the volunteer refuses.

The watchman starts to get back into the sack containing his bottle of red wine. Mrs. Domarkienė rolls her eyes a little, nudges her glasses off her nose, and gives the watchman one of her steely glances. She goes into her big purse and brings out a small glass bottle filled with milk. She peels off the foil cap and hands the bottle to the watchman, who holds it lightly in his hand, scowling, until she stabs him in his ribs with her elbow. The watchman scowls a little more then tips the milk to his lips. He quickly hands it back to Mrs. Domarkienė and wipes the milk from his beard stubble with his forearm. He lifts his eyes skyward.

"It will snow today," the watchman says. His chin dips and he begins to drowse.

Mrs. Domarkienė hands the bottle of milk to the volunteer. "It's our milk," she says, "like mother's milk, yes?"

The milk tastes warm and sweet, sweeter than he's ever remembered milk could be, but he's irritated by her question. How is he to remember his own mother's milk?

"Last night," he confesses, "I went to the old Manor House. I went through the trees to the ruined playground. I saw the three children there," then adds, "singing to a cow."

"They are *raudai*," she says, "songs orphans sing for the ones they've lost."

The volunteer looks beyond the road for some sign of the children.

"There must be something I can do," the volunteer says.

"Why don't you relax?" Mrs. Domarkienė says. "You know, work will wait. It is not like a wolf that will run into the trees." She sidles a foot or so along the rim of the fountain and points at the space she's created for him. "Sit!" she says, her eyes wild and green. She smacks the lip of the fountain with her flattened palm. "Right here." Her glasses slide to the tip of her nose. "Just. Sit. Down!"

And now—it is now—that the volunteer sits with the others. A simple task. To sit. He can scarcely believe it.

"You know," Mrs. Domarkienė says, "you are the very first American we have met. The very first. Ever."

The sun ripens above the horizon. The sky above the horizon is sanguine, washes out memory of the ruined playground, the green fire, and pale afternoon moon. An evening breeze stiffens and flattens the fountain spray to one side. It tears droplets from the stream and scatters them over the basin, onto three astonished faces.

The watchman starts from his silken slumber, holds his palms to the sky.

"So, what now?" he says and falls back asleep.

The Deposition of Jadwiga Dobilas to the Military Delegation, 16 August 1834

Inspired by Saulius Sužiedėlis's translation of a document from the Diocesan Archive of Łomża

Sirs, I knew Jósef Dobilas before I married Adam Adamczyk. I knew him long before my children with Adam were born, and long before Adam died. I knew Jósef when we were children in Gordzie, schoolmates. Years passed before I saw Jósef again just before Pentecost of this year. I went into the forest to pick mushrooms. It was about dusk. In the distance someone was burning brush and blue smoke was drifting through the pines. It was quiet and hazy, but I was able to see Jósef leaning against a pine tree, holding a foot up with one hand and tightening the leggings of his birch sandal with the other. I was in a hurry—night was coming on—so I turned to go. I startled Jósef. He gasped, dropped his foot to the ground, and jumped behind the tree. I saw a bit of his face—one eye—peer at me next to the bark. He recognized me.

"Jadwiga," he called. "Where are you going?"

I came a bit closer to him and saw he wore only a light vest for such a chilly evening. He started to shiver.

"I'm sorry I frightened you," I said. "I thought you were in the Polish Army."

He revealed a little more of himself, a hand, elbow, one ragged lapel of his shirt.

"I was," he replied and removed a small flask of midus from the pocket of his vest. "After the fall of Warsaw, I returned to my family in Gordzie, but my sister, fearing harassment from the Polish Military Delegation, kept my holding in the farm and sent me away."

The sun went down and it was getting dark. I could scarcely make out his features. I told Jósef I had to go—but he went on with his story. He looked only like a dark shape, speaking, one leg up, one hand again adjusting his sandal so it made a rasping sound in the forest.

"You understand, right? I'd already fought in the insurrection against the Czar. And then to be drafted by the new Polish government installed by the Russians?" Finally, he let his leg drop. "Anyway, I went to the Russian Empire and wandered there for two years."

Jósef started to advance on me from the tree, but I took two small steps back and said. "What did you do in Russia?"

He stuck an elbow on the tree and leaned there, then went on.

"I wanted to do many things," he said and scratched his head. "But there were thieves and people of low moral character there. It is difficult. You know how things are. Besides—the Russians wanted to draft me."

"The Russians?"

By now almost all of his features were obscured by the lack of light. I could see only the ghost image of Józef, something that reminded of what a mother in our village once said to her son who was about to be drafted by the Russians—

Dear child, foreign soil will cover your bones,
so I will mourn you now—while you are home . . .

"Yes, Russians!" he went on. "But I deserted and returned and now I have been living in these woods by any means possible, trying to avoid the Polish Military Delegation. . . . Russians. Polish. Now it's all the same thing. War everywhere."

Sirs, I felt sorry for Józef and told him to begin distilling pine tar in the woods for income. In the meantime, I explained, I would secretly provide him with food. I know it was wrong, but what woman would not show pity for a man hunted by two empires? I believe he suffered greatly from many travails. Anyway, sirs, in a way I did regret telling Józef that I would help him survive in the forest. I was not sure how I could provide for him and my two children from my marriage with Adam Adamczyk who now lived with my old mother.

The next day I went into the village to sell the mushrooms I'd gathered. While on the road entering the village, I paused a moment to let the wagons pass. I suppose I just stopped the way people sometimes stop to rest a little. As one wagon passed, the pink snout of a pig poked out the bed, barely breathing, destined for the knife. Above the sideboards, its round wild eye rolled about in bewilderment and terror. When another wagon passed, out popped the drooping heads of ducks, geese, and chickens, also heading for the knife. But it wasn't the two wagons passing that changed my regret about helping Józef. It was the third wagon, overloaded, a girl sitting atop a swaying mountain of grain fresh from the fields. She wore a white kerchief on top of her head. She seemed so content, so happy, and she was smiling at me—me! Sirs, perhaps you know moments like this. One moment everything seems so hopeless, the next everything seems all right. You begin to believe that every scrap of food may be stretched impossibly far, even enough for Józef.

After this, I went to Józef's farm to visit his sister, who provided a little rye bread (extended with potatoes) and some gira. His sister didn't ask about Józef's condition. She didn't say anything. She simply gathered the provisions and handed them to me. The rest of Józef's food I got from begging.

Most days I got food to Jósef just before dawn. I took it upon myself to be the first to rise in the household of my master, Rifleman Mnich. I slept on top of the stove, so it was simple for me to get up, remove my bedding, and light the wood splinter. I took the bucket, and then went out for water, but extended my stay near the steam at the location Jósef and I agreed to meet. I delivered Jósef's food. By the time I returned to the Mnich homestead with the water, a cold light was seeping through cracks in the door and windows. Rifleman Mnich's niece was starting the bacon. I handed her the water for the potatoes.

"Sun's already up," she chided me. I had to hurry in the days that followed to keep Jósef safe.

Next time I visited Jósef in the forest, he was again leaning on a tree, this time a birch, chewing on a twig, his new woolen coat and leather leggings I'd gotten from his sister wrapped about him.

"Have you any tar for me to take into town?" I asked him.

He stared at me a long time then tossed the chewed twig aside. He kept looking at me and beyond me, the whites of his eyes big and wet. I couldn't get the image of the pig's eyes going to the slaughter out of my mind.

"What food have you brought?" he said.

I removed a hard sausage and some black bread from my pockets. He snatched them away, sat, and began to eat. "Marry me," he said, while chewing.

"Marry a deserter?" I replied, astonished. I kept looking at the sausage in his hand. Half of it I'd wanted to deliver to my mother and children.

"Your orphans need a father," he smiled.

"They don't need to be orphaned twice!"

"Don't worry," he went on, "you can get my share of the farm from my sister and use it to persuade Headman Krol to approach the Military Delegation with a waiver for me from the draft."

"Will it work?"

"No problem. Besides, your orphaned children . . ."

I'd thought about choosing a husband from among those few who were not conscripted, perhaps even one who may have mutilated himself, chopped off fingers or a hand to avoid military service. I supposed I would not find another physically able husband soon.

I went immediately to Borkowski, a servant at the Mnich homestead, and asked him to go with my future husband to find a pastor in Sapieżyszki. For the pastor's services, I gave Jósef and Borkowski three złoty I had gotten from Jósef's sister.

Later that evening, both men returned and, as agreed, we all met by the stream. Both men were very drunk. Their clothes were soaked from falling into the stream.

"The pastor," Jósef said, his back on the ground, eyes closed, face up. "He would not see us. Such times we live in. Such people! We were so disappointed. We went to a tavern . . ."

"And the three złoty I gave you?"

Jósef then began to curse his sister—called her by a terrible name—followed by something about her being the only woman he'd ever known to inherit a man's fortune. Then he rolled over on his face and slept. I sent Borkowski away. Then I removed my future husband's clothes, made a fire, and dried them—being sure to cover him with my cloak while I waited for them to dry.

After that, I went to Sapieżyszki myself and found Father Mackiewicz, the curate there, who said he hadn't known anything about two men coming earlier to see him, only that there had

been some loud drunken disturbance outside the church caused by two men. But he couldn't imagine it was related. When I told Father Mackiewicz about my orphaned children and Jósef living in the forest and our plans to wed, he graciously agreed to conduct the ceremony free of charge. Father Mackiewicz accompanied me into the forest. When we came upon Jósef, he was lying on one side of his face in the tall grass near the pine tree where I'd first met him. A bit of drool had formed at one corner of his mouth and ran down into the grass. Father knelt beside him and rousted him. Poor Jósef shivered like a newborn lamb when he saw Father.

"Oh, I'm sorry!" Jósef said, seeming to recognize Father, and leapt to his feet.

"It's alright, Jósef," Father whispered. "Jadwiga has explained everything."

"Everything?" Jósef gasped.

"Yes—you want to be married, don't you?"

"Uh, er, yes," Joseph mumbled, sighing with relief like wind through trees.

I gave the names of Agata and Tadenz Jajko as witnesses, although they were not present. It was then that Father Mackiewicz wedded me to Jósef Dobilas.

That evening I went secretly with Jósef to the granary of Rifleman Mnich where we spent the night together and completed our marriage contract.

Not long after we were married, but before Jósef had distilled any tar in the woods at all, he was arrested while stealing food from Rifleman Mnich's household. Borkowski found me in the pasture bringing a midday snack to some of the workers. By the time I got to the main house where they were detaining my husband, two soldiers were escorting him along the road into the forest.

I knew the soldiers would be taking him to Mariampol for his trial—and prison—or worse. Against my better judgment I went to see Rifleman Mnich, for I could have been discharged from service in his household for secretly marrying Jósef Dobilas. But when I told him, he was kind and did not discharge me. He was standing by the hearth, lighting his pipe. I heard him sucking hard on the pipe and watched the smoke float toward the ceiling in tiny clouds that flattened and vanished.

"Can my husband be executed?" I asked my master in a panic.

"He has evaded the draft—and committed other crimes," he said. Then he paused, removed his pipe from his mouth, and rested it in his hand at his hip. "It is likely he will only serve a short term in prison, then his military service." Then his voice changed from reassuring to stern. "But if your husband escapes from authorities again and is recaptured he will certainly be put to death."

I thanked Rifleman Mnich and quickly departed to follow the two soldiers and my husband on the road to Mariampol. I followed the three men all the way to Gryszkabuda, where they entered a tavern. When I entered the tavern myself, I noticed my husband sitting in the corner with the two soldiers. A moment they were all three looking at me, then they put their eyes down to their drinks—vodkas all—and began talking and laughing.

I approached them and said to Jósef, "I see you have at least twenty thaler there. Where did you get that kind of money?"

"From my dear sister—my share of the farm." He grunted and one of the soldiers laughed. "And from other sources—with the help of aitvaras!"

"You already have your share?" I asked. But my husband did not answer, so I went on. "I am happy for your good fortune, husband," I said. "May I have a few złoty to support my children?"

His eyes rolled sideways in his head. One of the soldiers nudged him in a knowing way. Then with a disdainful face, my husband slid three złoty across the table in my direction.

"You're happy," he said, "at my misfortune. And now you want my last grosz."

"Of course not!" I said, so loudly that the soldier on my husband's right took a bit of vodka up his nose and sneezed.

"Husband, if you'll give me a little more, I can use the money to approach Headman Krol and the Military Delegation about your waiver from the draft."

That was when my husband ordered me to buy vodka for him and the two soldiers with the entire three złoty he'd just given me for the children.

"No!" I said, but the soldiers' stares were so cold and menacing, I thought the soldiers might somehow harm Jósef. I ordered their drinks and paid and stood there, watching.

They were all well into their cups when a young woman came up to my husband and in my presence spoke to him:

"Jósef!" she said, laughing, almost howling. "Don't you know me? I am your cousin."

"You might be my cousin," my husband laughed, "but our family is large around here." He patted the seat next to him. "Sit down," he said. "We'll have some fun."

Sirs, when I left the tavern in Gryszkabuda for home I felt sure that neither my orphaned children nor I would ever see Jósef Dobilas again. Walking among the pines, where it is so quiet, as though one is in a church, one can let one's heart walk out and not worry whether it will return; after awhile one doesn't care; there's too much war; one can only hope the wandering heart will not die too far from home.

Well, sirs, I don't know who that young woman was in the tavern, or why she should know my husband, and I don't see that you've asked, so I'll go on to say that it was there, in that pine wood, my heart walking away as I described, that I made my mind up I would continue to support my children from the household of Rifleman Mnich—and from begging—until word came about my husband's fate—a prison term no doubt, military service no doubt. But I would wait. What else could I do? All this I accepted. A peace came over me that I cannot explain.

Several days passed, and then one day while I was drawing water from the stream near the Mnich homestead, just after dusk, there he was—my husband, Jósef Dobilas—crouching on a rock nearby, like a toad, his knees up, and smiling through his beard.

"How did you get free of the soldiers?" I asked him. He did not answer and instead hopped down from his rock. "Who was that woman in the tavern?" He remained silent, knelt, and began tugging at the laces of his new boots. "And where did you get those boots?"

"Bring me some food," he commanded.

Well, sirs, this was the very moment the Military Delegation—that is, you—arrived at the homestead of Rifleman Mnich. Jósef and I heard your horses, and so moved into the tall thistles near the stream and listened while you made inquiries about my husband's whereabouts.

The hour was late, and eventually the crickets began to bleat so loudly that my husband complained he could not hear what you were saying or where you might be moving to search for him—and so he ran downstream and into the forest, commanding again, with is last breath, "Don't forget my food. Bring it to the usual place!"

Sirs, I continued to listen to your inquiries, then heard one of you say my husband was sentenced to death, then say, "Poor devil." I couldn't have been mistaken, for those words, "poor devil," must have already been in my head waiting for you to set the same words adrift on the night air.

Sirs, these are terrible times. When I go to market I no longer see meat for my children. Yet I see the wild eyes of beasts condemned to slaughter, meant to feed others better off. I hear all around people say, "Nowadays, sacrifices must be made." I hear it in town, "war," whispered after meals, "more death." I see it on the faces of children who run in the streets. "Sacrifices"—I see it in the faces of women without men, men like Jósef without countries, without souls. Sirs, I know that my husband has been condemned to die, though I must admit, like you, I hardly know him—or that woman at the tavern. That is why I will risk your thinking I am not a loyal wife, because I know, as you know, that in these times sacrifices must be made. That is why I will take you to his hiding place, where I first startled Jósef Dobilas while I was picking mushrooms this past Pentecost. I will take you there, in hopes that after arresting him, after hearing my deposition that you, God help me, knowing my husband's character, and considering my needs and the needs of my orphaned children for a good, faithful, God-fearing husband and provider, that you, that the new government, God help me, will quickly, very quickly, mercifully and without further delay, once and for all and forever, release Jósef Dobilas, poor devil, from all his earthly travails . . .

-Read, accepted, and signed by Jadwiga Dobilas, XXX,
16 August 1834

74

Potter's Hovel

When Paul Rood arrived at the hovel in the birch wood near the Hill of Witches, he found animal prints in smooth, fleshy mud covered by standing water. The tracks appeared to have been made only shortly before his arrival, a set of roe prints straight through a ring of cold black ashes, site of an old fire. Other prints, those of a wolf or wild dog, circled the fire site. These second prints suggested that the roe had been frightened off by whatever had made them.

But who could be certain of anything? The former Young Pioneers Camp had been full-up, a place Rood believed he could count on for a night's rest, and all he could be sure of now was the rich scent of dark beer on the paršiukas driver's breath.

"Night comes," the driver said, handed him a small, bluish key, and pointed to the hovel which set at the end of a narrow sandy path through the birch trees. "Stay there. I will return in the morning to take you to the Thomas Mann Haus in Nida."

Even from its outer appearance the hovel might have been more: gray pine sideboards were splotched with pink and white molds and green lichen, some like coral fans spreading from seams in the rotting wood; and the roof was hay-thatched, charming, if not rankled into prickly shafts of straw sprouting all angles along the bowed and failing center beam.

He worked his key into the old Soviet lock until the jaws dropped, removed the lock from the latch, pushed the door inward and stepped inside. The door drifted back, half shut, and rocked a little on its hinges. He shut the door and removed a candle from his bag, stuck it into a knothole in the floor planks, knelt, and lit the wick. The flame took immediately and grew until it illuminated three large piles of pottery shards in three corners of the room. In the fourth corner lay a sack mattress stuffed with straw.

Rood removed a fragment from one pile of the broken pots, what might have been a shallow bowl. He poured a little wax from the candle onto it, set the butt of the candle in the soft wax, and carried the shard, candle affixed, hip level, to examine the other piles of broken pottery.

The shards, all gray, earthen and unfired, were all sorts and shapes, most angular, edgy, dead. In one pile the fragments were broken shallow plates or bowls piled densely on top of one another; in another, the shards were thicker, more curved and rose in long, vertical shapes, as if from tall, pendulous pitchers; the height of the third pile was somewhere between the former two and the shards seemed to curve sharply outward, horizontally; among these pieces were others poking out, pieces from what might have been bulbous flasks, their stomachs broken open.

Some mad artist?

Or Soviet soldiers on their way out, south to Kalingrad, smashing things . . .

When light left the birch wood of the Hill of Witches the moon came up, pouring silvery light through the small window of the hovel; the light came and went as small clouds passed through the sky.

Rood cleared away some of the pottery fragments near the straw sack and settled into it.

Then he got up.

He blew out the candle.

He returned to the straw sack, followed by his long shadow, drawn in the moonlight across the floor planks of the hovel.

He lay down and dozed.

Near dawn, he woke when he heard something move outside the window.

He waited for the sound to go away and for sleep.

Then he saw the boy's face, framed by the window—a thin face, darkly complected, short dark hair, and large, round eyes with astonishing blue-moon centers.

"Raganos!" the boy shouted.

Witches.

Rood got up and went to the window, but the boy's face, those eyes, blue moons, disappeared from the window frame; then he heard the boy's fists beating the opposite wall outside.

"Raganos! Raganos!"

The boy pounded so hard that the unfired shards against three walls of the hovel rattled in dead chords against the floorboards.

Rood opened the door and walked out the hovel, then around to its rear where he found the boy squatting behind a fern with long, tongue-like fronds, heavy with new dew. The boy wore loosely fitting white cotton pajamas, rubber thongs on his feet, no socks, and he held his face in his hands. He did not seem to notice Rood. Then the boy raised his head and removed his hands from his face. Rood saw that he was thin, perhaps not more than nine years of age, but old-seeming, ashen in the face, except for those eyes, which shone blue in the weak light, out from deep sockets.

"Witches?" Rood said. "Raganos?"

The boy pointed in the direction of the animal prints in the mud around the dark ashen circle in front of the hovel.

"Are you from the Young Pioneers Camp? Do you understand? Young Pioneers?"

"Taip," the boy replied.

"Then, listen. . . . I will take you back to the Camp when the light is better. Morning. *Rytas*. You understand?"

"Taip."

The boy followed him into the hovel and squatted in one corner near the pile of shallow shards. Then the boy pointed, one at a time, to each corner, to each pile of shards.

"Raganos," the boy said.

"Ne raganos," Rood replied.

The boy sat on the floor among the gray shards and began to rock sightly, to and fro, and Rood went back to his sack and slept with the boy like that, rocking.

Rood woke and the hovel was drenched with opaque morning light.

The boy had reconstructed one of the pots, a flask with a protuberant belly. Rood knelt by the boy and examined the pot closely. The lines along which the pot had broken were long, smooth, not what Rood would have thought. Not jagged. And the pot was larger than he would have expected. It might have held at least ten liters.

"Labai gerai," Rood said to the boy, who began to work on a second reconstruction in another corner of the hovel.

Rood stepped outside and saw that the collage of animal prints had been complicated by prints of the boy's rubber thongs. Raganos. The boy must have been frantic; the mud was riddled with signs of his running about.

Rood went back to the hovel, leaned inside the doorjamb and motioned for the boy to come outside. But the boy did not look up from his second reconstruction.

"Come on," Rood said. "I'll show you your witches." But the boy who had apparently strayed from the Young Pioneers Camp continued to squat among the fragments. Rood watched the boy pick up one shard and run his index finger along the line of the break in a shallow bowl. He removed another piece from the pile and rubbed the two pieces together to see if the seams matched. He picked out a third fragment and began to compare it to the first. "All right," Rood said. "I'll be back a little later to take you to the Camp."

But Rood did not leave immediately. He continued to watch the boy work until he'd reconstructed another shallow bowl and a tall, slender urn. After finishing the urn, the boy walked to the straw sack, lay down, and closed his eyes. Then Rood left him, sleeping.

Clouds broke to pieces overhead. The sky cleared and grew blue-bright.

Rood walked in the direction of the Baltic Sea, up a small path that rose into the birch wood, until he found the intertwined osiers of willows laid lengthwise along the berms. He followed the woven osiers until beyond them he found the heavy, full blooms of pink and white bijūnai and strawberry-shaped lavender blossoms of dobilai. When he turned to look down the path in the direction of the hovel, he saw the boy coming up the hill. The boy was some distance back, so Rood motioned with his arm for the boy to come, to hurry, while he continued up, a little slower so the boy could catch him. But when he looked for the boy again, his distance from the boy had not diminished at all. And the boy had stopped when Rood turned to look.

Rood continued up the hill, where pines with long limbs reached across the narrowing path and the sky began to cloud quickly. More clouds with ragged bottoms flew in from the Baltic Sea, sweeping inland from the horizon until they sailed over Rood's head, throwing dark shadows over the steep hill as they passed. The dobilai and bijūnai eventually gave way to rūta, which thrived in sandy soil and low shaded areas. The delicate plant had small lime-green leaves, and was speckled with tiny, yellow flowers. He stopped to pick a spring of rūta and crushed its aromatic leaves between his fingers. A strong enough tea of rūta could cause hallucinations. Raganos! he thought and smiled.

The sun was nearly overhead when Rood came to carvings in the trunks of great pines, trunks bare and scribbled with names of lovers on summer solstices, couples seeking the papartis, the mythical flowering fern, to roll in the dew of its leaves, naked, to make their skins eternally smooth and young.

Here, at the carvings made by lovers, Rood strayed from the path to a stand of ferns where there were no miraculous flowers. But some plants still held a little dew in the intricate lattices of their curled leaves. He wetted his fingertips with the dew from a plant and spread it over his face. The dew was cool, startling, but not surprising—he'd been sweating the past few minutes walking up the hill.

Then through the ferns he saw the boy on the path, watching him with his blue-centered eyes. When Rood started forward the boy cried, "Raganos," and pointed at the ferns around Rood.

"Ne raganos!" Rood shouted and continued to walk toward the boy through the ferns, "Papartis."

And when Rood came a little closer to the boy, thick, dark clouds overhead grumbled.

"Perkūnas!" the frightened boy shouted.

Thunder god.

"Nera Perkūnas," Rood replied, looking at the sky. "Electricity."

But when he looked back to the boy he was gone—and when Rood reached the path, he could not see the boy either way along it.

By the time Rood reached the top of the hill, pines grew squat, round, their needles long and pale green. There, he found the carving he sought, a pagan totem of Neringa, image of an infant child carved under the figure of a king and queen—all made of one piece of pine still rooted in the ground, for along the Kuršių Spit tree roots grew over eight meters into the earth to keep trunks centered, to survive the winds and shifting sand of the dunes. The carving depicted the infant Neringa being brought to a childless king and queen by a magical deer. In later life Neringa would grow into a giantess and built the great dunes of Nida. . . . All this was so clear from the carving, what was left to do but to look at the sculptor's name?—I. Užkurnys—then to mount the very top of the hill, from where he could see all the sands of Nida and the Baltic Sea below, and the low black spots where the sands had drifted from shore, where amber diggers looked for ancient hard resins, proof of pre-human existence. A mosquito trapped forever in amber chambers. Hadn't he heard once it was likely that during his lifetime he'd breathe at least one molecule of oxygen that, say, Cleopatra or Alexander the Great might have breathed? Then wasn't it also likely he'd inhaled some molecule of oxygen first breathed by some prehistoric mosquito?

He looked at the sky, the line of trees over the violent sea swept by wind.

The sun came briefly out of the clouds.

It was directly overhead.

He had no shadow.

The briefest moment he was bathed in full light.

Noon—and he felt could hold the light, there, all around himself. Like magic.

Then the sun went behind a cloud and rain began.

In a little while, he had to turn back.

As Rood descended the hill, people and animals were coming up it. None of them seemed to mind the rain. A thin woman held a newspaper over her head. She carried a baby strapped to her chest, its arms and feet spread out like a turtle's, flopping slightly as the woman walked. An old man shuffled along with a cane. A large burn scar covered his right cheek; there was no expression on his face and no cover for his head. A young man and woman shared an umbrella and spoke Polish in tender, soft tones. A column of goslings followed a goose. . . . After they passed him, time to time he turned around to follow their progress: it seemed to him more than a strange concoction of pilgrims walking up a pagan hillside. They belonged to the hill, belonged as precisely as the papartis and the giantess who had created the dunes and trees with eight-meter roots . . .

By the time he returned to the hovel, the rain had stopped and the animal and human prints he'd seen around the ring of ashes—roe, wolf, boy—were all submerged by a thin layer of water, and the dry, gray wood of the hovel was dark from the dampness.

He opened the door to the hovel and found all the shards in three heaps as before, as if the small spaces the boy had enclosed with his reconstructions, bowl, urn, dish, had never existed.

The possibilities did not begin to cross his mind until he gathered his candles and set out for the main road to meet the driver of the paršiukas. The boy might have taken great care to take apart the vessels, piece by piece, and replaced the shards on the piles he had taken them from. But the piles seemed so like when he first arrived at the hovel. Shattered. Pointless. He had felt a kind of satisfaction when the boy had transformed the pieces of pots into what seemed their original forms. And now, this emptiness?

Real emptiness?

—or was it a trick of the mind?

Along the narrow path back to the main road, Rood watched a high, thin vapor trail divide the sky, its residual clouds sailing west and dispersing over the Baltic.

The driver of the paršiukas was waiting for him. The motor was running.

"You are late," the driver said, his breath heavy with a new round of beer. Rood shrugged his shoulders. The driver shrugged his shoulders back at him. "Kur?" he added.

"First to the Young Pioneers Camp," Rood replied. Then he pointed at the vapor trail in the sky over the Hill of Witches. "Raganos," he said and got into the paršiukas.

"Ne raganos," the driver laughed. "Avialinijos. . . . Perhaps you want to go home? Perhaps you want to go to the airport now?"

"Ne," Rood said, laughed, and pointed at the sky again. "Raganos."

The driver shook his head in disbelief and put the paršiukas in gear.

Later, when the driver dropped him at the Young Pioneers Camp, Rood's report of the boy at the potter's hovel appeared to be carefully recorded by the camp's Officer. More than one time the Officer's eyebrows lifted when Rood explained his strange encounter with the boy. Then Rood asked the Officer whether such a boy, wearing pajamas and rubber thongs, was missing from the Camp, yet he received only a silent stare.

"No English," the Officer said.

And Rood saw only blue lines on the Officer's paper, broken by small spaces where he had lifted his pen.

The Blue Room (Vilnius)

Mother, His Own Mother

Dead a week, ashes in a blue jar in Salt Lake, six thousand miles from Old Town Vilnius, too late to fly back, yet as he hobbled over high cobblestones to cross Pylimo Street, he felt her perch somewhere on his spine, felt her reach forward from his backbone and crawl along his ribs, then down, into his legs.

"Son," he could hear her, "don't slouch."

He stiffened his gait, paused when cut off by an old yellow trolley that groped forward, dynamo whining. Its taurus-like antennae snapped against overhead lines and sparked blue, like a strange mechanical bull, pregnant with day workers, long eyes that ran to mouths, shoulders, hips, eyes flowing downward, fetal eyes with fates tied to gravity.

When the trolley passed, he crossed Pylimo, turned onto Trakų. He passed a shoe store, in its display window KOLEKCIJA 'MARILYN MONROE,' blocked toes ramped up high black heels, so high he supposed anyone wearing the shoes would be inclined to tilt forward, both in the sense of gradient and predilection, and so he tipped forward, feeling just inches ahead of the feeling of his mother returning. At times he swept himself back, spine straight, abandoning his headlong teetering, and she caught him—his mother's half-smile, his; her slow gait, his; the muscle tick high on her left cheek.

"Son, life's too short," she said. "See the world!"

He tried to out-walk her, forty quick paces, forty had worked once before, forty and she'd let him go. So he headed for Vokiečių Street, stared at the toes of his shoes on the curb, a precipice that threatened to zoom up and swallow him. He swung right onto Vokiečių Street, one pace, four, five, his head down, seeing early spring water darkening cobblestones, daring him to stick a toe to an uneven edge and fall facedown into the street. He put his head up, eyes sallow, straight ahead. Fifteen more steps and he could feel his left leg, shorter than his right, tugging his hip left. Had she that same teeter-tottering gait? Shouldn't he remember? Impossible now. Dead. Ashes.

"Blue jar," his brother had said on the telephone. "Do you think blue is alright?"

"How blue?" he asked.

"Blue, blue," his brother said. "Very blue."

Fifteen paces more. His heart pounded in his neck. The final five, three, two.

He stopped, looked all about Vokiečių, once a street bereft of motion and color a decade before when Soviets pulled out of Lithuania, buildings now in colors of new capitalism, pastels of yellow, lavender, and white below buoyant red rooftops that seemed to unzip the radiant April sky at its edges, and let it pour out, down, onto the wide, verdant median that divided Vokiečių. Clean. Bright.

"Don't worry," her words before he went overseas, "you're an American," words to unfetter him, "try to have some fun."

And she'd let him go. No strings. No warnings. No regrets. But where should he go now? Now that she had gone out of the world? He watched two intertwined clouds rope upward over the Town Hall, vestiges of a vapor trail, an air show earlier that featured the President of Lithuania, Paksas, a seasoned pilot who flew his resurrected World War Two fighter plane under the Kalvarijų bridge over the Nemunas River, hauling a long banner, words in Lithuanian and English, PAKSAS: A NEW DIREC-TION! A sign. Just what he needed. He veered onto the median, into the first beer tent of spring, empire blue, dull, greenish blue, color of summer lilacs that had overrun his mother's wild roses.

"Jesus, Mary, and Joseph!" she'd declared. "Soon the world will be crawling with my little blue trumpets!"

He dragged a wire chair up to a plastic table, noting its scuffing sound, strange, like what? Pity? Scuffing pity. The reason she may have taken possession of him so suddenly on Pylimo while the long-eyed trolley people lumbered by? He'd not seen his mother the last five years of her life, and the other thirty she'd been so alone, her husband having died young, 1976, only two years after NASA laid him off. No more Apollo. No more Moon. Instead, her depression. Medications. Switching medications. Doctors. Switching doctors. Money. More money. No more reaching into outer space. Yet now he could feel her reaching. Silly thoughts. Silly big wide world. Silly fears. Still.

He ordered a Švyturys beer from the new girl, young, must have been in her teens, complexion like heavy cream, blue headband tugging severely at her dirty blond hair, dark at its roots. She smiled at him, a discretion-ary smile, like his mother's smile. He smiled politely when the barmaid walked up with his draft.

"Ačiū," he said.

"You are welcome," she said. She pinched the tall beer glass between two fingers, and lowered it in front of him. "Speak English," she added. "I need the practice." A color like mascara bled into her eyes, as if sadness were a liquid that ran out of one's forehead and into the eyes, like gun-blue, a color with dark light trapped inside, a color that seemed to echo her words, "English is our other mother tongue."

"Say that ten times fast."

"Say what?"

"Other mother tongue. Other mother tongue . . . ten times."

The barmaid winced, turned on a heel and left. He sipped his beer, amber, a little red, good beer that cut through things and went straight to the matter of easing one into a chair, table, place, settling the stomach and casting a net of new feelings over him. When he set the cool glass back on the table, he breathed deeply and thought about the new barmaid. He'd seen her before, perhaps at Lithuania's first superstore, Maxima's, next to the barrel of dried herring and the huge high-tech TROPICANA U.S.A. juicer that looked like a locomotive engine tilted at the ceiling.

He finished the Švyturys, got up, and stepped outside the blue tent. A small man, his face dark with stubble, staggered out of a jeweler's shop and into him.

"Mister American," the man panted. He shoved a Rolex in his face. "A thousand litai—please!"

The thief looked left, right, then ran off, passing a freshly painted mural, a tropical undersea world, complete with moray eels lurking, silvery striped bass, barracuda, sharks, and assorted smaller denizens of orange, yellow, and blue. 'VEGAS' CASINO EXOTICA the sign said. NAUJOJA!—"New!" he smiled to himself. Not so, he thought. Only new in Lithuania. He watched the thief dash into an alley that led to the BROADWAY nightclub, then he wandered back onto the wide grassy median of Vokiečių, drifting among green benches, where people strolled, sat or lay on the lawn—the spring air drew them out in colorful clothes— reds, greens, yellows. It dazzled him to see people at such ease. He believed he could walk forever, that any street would lead him to infinite intercon- nected streets, and that these boundless streets might lead him anywhere.

When he reached the opposite side of Vokiečių he passed what had been a wine shop. Within the frame of the broad street window, row after row of Lithuanian women sat in folding chairs paying close attention to a tall American woman, her long red-nailed fingers folded over the yellow fluted lid of a plastic bowl. She popped it open, snapped it closed. Pop! Snap! She repeated. His mother again? No, this time American Tupperware. In Lithuania. Snap! Pop! He walked faster, turned left onto Rotušes, passed a chemist's shop, noticed a bill posted on a lamppost: DEPRESIJA KON- FERENCIJA—sponsored by Eli Lilly Corporation, "Introducing Pro- zac," and another posted underneath, ANNUAL SUICIDE MEETING, co-sponsored by Lilly. By the time Rotušes gave over to Didžioji Street, the air suddenly warmed and he felt heat rise along his neck, sweat, then an odd cooling sensation—mother? Had she found him in Vilnius, along with Lilly? Signs. Each step reminders. Depression. Suicide. Just signs. Meant nothing. Blue ashes. Still.

He passed the Orthodox Church of Saint Nicholas the Wonder Worker, complete with its rotund chapel built in honor of the Hangman of Vilnius, one General Mikhail Muravyev, responsible for stringing up leaders of the 1863 Lithuanian revolt against the Czar. A wonder the Hangman is remembered, and so notoriously visible after so much time! From there he made his way down Pilies Street through the mugė, where he was surprised to see a new popular item of sidewalk sellers—the Worried Christ, Christ upon a slouching wooden throne, his head tilted to one side, resting on weary hands, hair unkempt, stringy, eyes puffed with the dark stuff of insomnia. Row after row of molded plastic Christs sat before him, all in rank, many sizes, seven inches to three feet tall. So many Worried Saviors! He bought a small one, clutched it tightly in his right hand, so the Christ's head showed above the first knuckle of his fist.

He swerved right, across Pilies and onto the triangle, skirting other tents in front of the Church of Paraskovila Piatnickaya, its big copper top, then found himself ensnared in swinging leather purses, briefcases, all manner of bags bumping him, price tags whirling and ticking about his ears, straps entwined about his elbows, like a jungle of thick-bladed plants. He swung the Worried Christ at the undergrowth, hacking with it like a mighty machete. He came out of the leather jungle, paused a few seconds to orient himself, then proceeded right onto Bokšto Street. At his rear, automobiles clattered over old brick, whining past, nearly at his elbow. He was nervous, traffic so close, but he liked streets like Bokšto, narrow, untidy, undemanding streets with sad, neglected histories, streets so preoccupied with the past that they bothered no one, and instead brooded in angular, deep, purplish shadows.

He turned right onto Sąvičiaus Street, passed the old abandoned church, its iron fence festooned with rusted barbed wire, plastered walls brown and tannic with age. He paused outside the fence and looked skyward for the empty iron u-clamps that once held the bell in place in the tower, now mouthless, clapperless, tongueless.

"Well?" he said aloud and looked at the sad eyes of the silent Christ. "What now?"

"Jesus," his mother would have replied, "you worry too much!"

He walked farther along Sąvičiaus, past a polished tin sign inscribed STRANGE MONK KAVINĖ, until he found the gate and tunnel to the courtyard of his apartment building. Even in strong sunlight the tunnel was very dark. He wasn't afraid of being attacked inside. He could defend himself.

"You were a big baby!" his mother was fond of saying, a little wince of pain on her face in memory of her prolonged labor with him.

But the water in the dark tunnel paralyzed him. Even after days of dry weather the unevenly cobbled bricks of the tunnel held pools of dirty water that had run down the outsides of old buildings. What if he tripped, thrown head-first into the filthy water? He took a penlight out of his pocket, pointed it at the bricks, began to navigate around pools. Once, the toe of his shoe touched the black liquid. He withdrew it, shaking it like the paw of a hydrophobic cat.

In light at the other end of the tunnel he spotted his neighbor, a gray balding man he suspected with former-KGB ties, judging by the bulletproof glass enclosing his entryway. He could hear echoes of the man's hurried footsteps knocking off the brick walls of the courtyard. He glimpsed him scurry into his black Mercedes, start it, and enter the tunnel. He heard dirty black water piling against the Mercedes's sidewalls, sloshing over bricks. Then the dreadnought raced by him, throwing dark waves of filth onto his trousers! He backed out of the tunnel, wincing in the obscene afternoon light glancing off the tin shingle of the STRANGE MONK. He stood, red-knuckled against the abrasive plaster of the archway.

"Look at your pants!" he could hear her saying.

He fled, down Sąvičiaus, then Didžioji. Five—fifteen paces—twenty— forty to again shake the feeling of her—and found himself on his way back to the blue beer tent on Vokiečių. When he arrived, he sat at the same table, set the Worried Christ in front of him, and the same barmaid came over, her black roots, dark liquid light trapped in her eyes.

"Švyturys," he grumbled.

The barmaid eyed the dark stains on his trousers, then brought him a tall beer, taller than before, the sides of the glass sweating so beautifully that he caressed the condensation lovingly with a fingertip, shook off a bit of water, then put his mouth to the task of downing the beer with one long swallow.

"More," he commanded the barmaid.

"More?" she said, parking one hip against the edge of his table, her eyes on the slips of beer draining down the insides of his empty glass.

"You said you wanted to learn English." He tilted the mouth of the glass so she could peer inside. "Well, the first and most important American word to know is 'more.' Understand? More, more, more." The barmaid leaned a little more on his table, an expression of expectation on her face—open, waiting for him to say *more* once more! "More. Say it ten times fast." He burped and nodded at the Worried Christ. "And bring one for him."

"Him?"

When he laughed, she smiled and went off for his beer.

When she returned, she set two tall glasses in front of him. "There you are," she said. "More." She leaned a little on the table again. "As you Americans say." She smiled, what seemed wickedly, the dark liquid in her eyes seeming to glow. "Better?"

That *was* better, he mused. "Okay, try this one. Say *Amerikiečių* ten times fast."

"*American?*"

"Yes."

The barmaid grew a wry smile, complied, and upon her tenth utterance declared, "Well, that fast, *Amerikiečių* sounds like *I'm-here-to-get-you.*"

"Congratulations," he said, "you've mastered American English!"

He gloated over his small victory by running his fingertips over the outside of his glass, collecting droplets of water that ran down his fingers onto the roof of his palm, fell to the oilcloth, and formed a little puddle at the toes poking out the Worried Christ's plastic sandals. The barmaid stood a while watching him, then left before he'd finished telling her, "No more English lessons today," but not before he could feel his mother again, in his fingers as they gathered more condensate, feel her blood pulsing to the surface of each fingertip when she stopped the point of her sewing needle with her steel thimble. When he raised his arm to gulp his beer, he sensed her arms, draped with wet clothes, mouth stuffed with wooden clothes pins. He could feel his expression, half his in Lithuania; half his mother's in America; his face quivering somewhere between cold and warm, between early spring and late summer; mouth half snarl, half smile.

When he staggered out the blue tent on Vokiečių, the bluer night was coming on. By the time he turned the corner onto Didžioji, an even bluer night fell silent. He would not return to his flat on Sąvičiaus. He began his long uncertain walk to an older, darker part of the city, while stars blazed forth as though no expanse of torpid sky dare hold them back.

Scenes from a Green Bench in Vilnius

1. Mother and Daughter

An airplane drones in a blue summer sky, lugs a banner that trails back ten times the length of the plane, letters in bright blue.

NATO FOR NATIONAL SECURITY

He sits on a green bench in the grassy median of Vokiečių Street, sets a bouquet of six red roses aside, and watches the banner pass behind a bright yellow building opposite the bench.

In a short while, two women sit together on the far end of the same bench. He listens to their conversation in Lithuanian, understands only fragments:

> daughter, in Soviet times our flat cost *nothing*
> mother, *nothing* is free
> daughter, how to pay my electric bill?
> show you sometime
> how to pay my taxes?
> I *will* show you sometime
> daughter, you are so busy?
> now we rent cars *and* rooms
> you are so busy
> …
> mother
> what?
> oh, mother
> what?
> oh, *nothing*, just *mother*!

2. Varnai

Varnai waddle about the green bench, large black birds with thick, downy gray wings like winter coats. People scatter rye bread for the varnai, which make a show of ignoring the scraps. Then, when no one seems to look, they hop to a crust, peck it up, and continue waddling, as if nothing in the world has changed, or ever will.

3. Turtle Baby

A young woman with a baby strapped on her back approaches the green bench, heaving away at the sack containing the child, first one shoulder, then the other. Each time she hefts the child to reposition the straps on her shoulders, the baby's arms flop to one side or the other, dragging one or the other strap off a shoulder. Light from the sun low over the rooftops reflects off the woman's eyeglasses, and she seems to be looking into the eyes of the man on the green bench, searching them as if she knows him.

But as she draws closer, the angle of sunlight changes and she continues toward him without glint or trick of recognition.

Such beautiful morning light. "Labaryta!" he says.

The woman tilts a bit forward, gasps, and passes the man on the bench; her baby's arms flop out its back sack like turtle legs out an old shell, arms flailing at him in mocking infantile applause.

4. Old Boots

A tiny old woman carries a plain cardboard box, wears an empire blue dress and pair of old dull-black Russian boots. She sits on the green bench, fusses with her purse, removes a small paper sack containing scraps of dark bread. Pigeons waddle her way en masse, necks up and down, sounds, roo-koo, wak-wak. She flings the bread in broad strokes, like an orchestra conductor, moves one arm in crescendo, then, realizing she grows short of scraps, presses down with the palm of the other, as in pianissimo, yet the birds ignore her plea—roo-koo! wak-wak, each bird insisting on its share—and more.

She tosses the empty sack at a purple-white pigeon, its breast spotted with mud splatter.

"Palikite mane ramybėje!" she says then tosses the empty sack at the bird and kicks at it with the toe of her boot.

Pigeons comply with her wish to be left alone, roo-koo! wak-wak, bob and scatter. Then she stares at the toe of one Russian boot a good while, reaches down, snags it in one palm and lifts it to rest on her other leg. She takes the heel in one hand and tries to remove the boot, but it won't budge. She opens the box and removes a new pair of sandals, tries the boot again unsuccessfully, glances sideways at her companion on the bench, says "Prašom," but before he can respond to her plea for help, an officer in the Lithuania army intervenes and, without a word, seizes the troublesome Russian boot, sticks a leg to the bench for leverage, and hauls back on the boot with such force that the tiny woman flies off the green bench, bounces on her derriere on the gassy ground, and lies at the feet of the startled officer, who scrambles to assist her, at which point she kicks his shin.

"Palikite mane ramybėje!" she grumbles.

"Roo-koo! wak-wak," reply the laughing pigeons.

5. Rain

When rain comes, the man does not move from the green bench—it is a thin, short rain that sweeps across the median with a single swish. When sunlight returns, he spies a single crack in the bright yellow building. It slants from eave to foundation, jagged, like a lightning strike.

6. Vilma

She arrives, a young, thin woman in a tweed skirt, silken blouse billowing about her in a morning breeze, a round timepiece she keeps on a gold chain swinging about her neck. When she sits next to him on the green bench, he takes up the bouquet of six red roses and hands it to her.

"English all the way?" he says.

"Yes, English," she replies, takes the roses. "Thank you," she adds. "How nice of you to remember that today is International Women's Day."

"You're welcome," he says, smiling, though he had no idea it is a day to honor women.

The night before, he'd brought the same bouquet of roses to a bar on Totorių Street, BŪSI TREČIAS, but she had been with another woman, and so he hid them in the hat rack. When he joined the two women, Vilma said to him, "Hello!" Then she laughed. "Do you know what the name of this bar is in English?—YOU WILL BE THE THIRD ONE!"

Vilma snags her timepiece and holds it close to her face, then drops it to jostle at her neck. "So, shall we converse?"

"Yes," he says. "I was wondering, you know, if we even need so many languages at all. I mean, if you know the rules of things like football, or notes of music, then aren't different languages unnecessary?" He can see she is caressing her timepiece. "I mean all these different languages are like God's punishment, Tower of Babel, all that."

He can almost follow her eyes to the damp exterior of the bright yellow building and faint crack looking like a lightning strike. "Oh, you want to doubt the usefulness of languages," Vilma says, a wry line-smile spreading. "Well, I don't know English well enough to have this philosophical discussion!"

"Touché," he says.

"Tuščia?" She is obviously annoyed and shifts her weight forward, nearly off the bench. "What do you mean by 'You're empty?'"

"No—I mean, 'touché'—you have made a winning point in the game."

7. Mise-en-scène

Near the green bench, along the front of the bright yellow building, walks a man with a red shirt and green trousers. A white corgi follows him. When the man stops, the small dog collides with the man's legs, then looks left, right, up, down. One can see white fibrous cataracts in both eyes of the corgi. When the man proceeds again down the street, slowly, he repeats aloud at regular intervals a single-syllabled something to guide the dog behind him, a word indecipherable. It rains again, and afterward a child appears out an alley very near the green bench. He blows a single note on a small flute, over and over.

Blue

He says, "We probably know everything there is to know about one another."

She says, "There is so little we don't know."

The man and woman part.

They never see one another again.

Perhaps remarkable is the way they hug before they separate forever, her thin arms, high and lightly about his neck, forearms crossed, her hands gently touching his shoulder blades. His hands rest at her waist and pull her to him. They stand, just so, a short time, embracing silently, while above and all around it is midday blue, blue sky-wide and full of luminous depth, blue knowing no reason to tell their story forward—perhaps only backward—for it is a blue that won't be ignored.

She whispers to him, "They are still warplanes to me." She lowers her head. "The ones I remember. I don't care how you paint them now."

Before that he says, breathless, excitedly, "Look!" He points above the red, red, pantiles of a bread shop. "An air show!"

The buildings of Old Town Vilnius rumble and above them is an echoic clatter of engines droning, rattling windows. The streets tremble. Three freshly painted warplanes arc upward, then dive behind roofs buildings cutting the morning sky, and swoop back up in tight formation.

That morning they are on Pilies gatvė, a short distance from the Great Cathedral. Tall medieval buildings line the lane, freshly painted shades of lime and bone. Sharp shadows fall from the crests of several buildings. Gray, rhombic shapes shroud cobbled streets below.

She says, "Yes, I'll have coffee."

He smiles at the waiter, says, "No thanks," and smokes.

After a long stretch of silence, while they eat, she remarks, "The rain depresses me."

He shakes the water out of his hair and says, "Well, here we are, safe and sound."

Rain comes down hard and cold, filling streets, sweeping every manner of litter along the cobblestones into sewers along Algirdo gatvė.

"It is like there are limitless possibilities," she says.

"The sky," he says, "everywhere, so blue."

They gaze out the opening to her balcony where white and yellow mums in a planter under a blue sky are watching them back.

After they first make love they are naked, wide-mouthed, and wide-eyed in the blue light of the blue room reflecting in from the summer afternoon sky. She lies on her state bed with her knees up, a towel over her waist. He sits in one of the wooden chairs, arms hanging over the arm rests. His head is back and he is looking at the ceiling. Her head is propped with a pillow and she stares at a spot on the wall opposite the bed.

"My father was a partisan," she says. "He joined them against the Soviets in the forests of Merkinė. He was killed by KGB in 1946, before I was born. His name is engraved on the KGB museum: 'Prancis Benetis.'"

"My father was a physicist for the space program," he says. "After the moon landing, they laid him off and gave him a coin inscribed, 'One giant leap for Mankind.' He died shortly after that."

"My mother is bitter because she worked so hard when the communists were here—and now?"

"My mother had a breakdown when my father died."

They speak not in torrents but in the way a great division crumbles and waters of the past flow irreversibly together over a broken barrier. Waters piled so high so long against the stubborn stones of time that now they eagerly ebb, mingle, and flow together, but then apart . . .

"I train our military to use English," she says. "Military English. It is important for us to join NATO."

"I restore medieval cities," he says.

"And so you have come to Vilnius," she says, "from America."

He comes in with the newspaper, *Rytas*, and a bag full of sugary, yeast-scented bandelai he buys from a woman on Vilniaus gatvė across from the taksi stand off Gedimino prospect.

She makes coffee, sets the small table, and sits a long time on her state bed, blinking her eyes, feeling rested the first time in days.

He rises from the chair he has carried and planted next to her bed, and goes out for more bandelai.

Near morning, she puts a light on. Her eyes are open and looking at the blue wall, a spot of it illuminated by the ceiling light above the top frame of her door.

He watches her sleeping, her chest rise, fall, and rise, then switches the light off. Only a sliver of light remains in the room, cast through the open window.

She gets into bed, says, "Thank you. You are very kind."

"No," he whispers, "I don't think it's a strange request, really."

"You must think I'm crazy."

"Just try to get some sleep," he says. "Don't worry."

The sun is nearly set, buried behind tall, angular buildings of Old Town. Only its rays can be seen throwing light upward from an unseen horizon into a vibrant blue sky.

"My God, what a beautiful room," he says.

"Just watch me while I sleep," she says. "Just tonight. Okay?"

"I understand."

"I had my flat painted blue last week," she says. "I thought it would help. But when I saw it I was suddenly seized by a childhood fear I had during the war. I stood in the center of the room watching the walls a long time, all blue and beautiful. I suddenly realized that if I closed my eyes tonight I would die. I've had my eyes open for days. It's silly, I know."

Her flat at T. Vrublevskio is simple as most flats Old Town Vilnius. A narrow state bed sits in one corner by the window. There is a table, teapot, and two wooden-slatted chairs. A door leads to a small balcony, and there one can see a planter with yellow and white mums, newly bloomed. Their tops quake in the slight breeze. Beyond this, in view, are the Great Cathedral and its wide, white piazza.

In another part of the city, the back of his neck rests against the top rail of his bench in Lukšių Square. His head is cocked back. He is watching the clear blue sky. He does not blink.

She plants mum seedlings in the flower box on the balcony. A moment she gets dizzy, returns inside and closes the balcony door behind her.

Around his park bench, several pigeons coo and cluck. He reads the newspaper, then takes the top edge of it down and notices the sky. He rests the paper in his lap.

She stands with her back to the balcony door of her flat. The room is painted freshly, blue. She pauses and stares at her walls. She does not blink.

Before this there was always blue. Not blueness that carries their spirits to far places. Not blueness within which their minds wander from what they will do, have done, or do. Blue that is blue. Blue, the color blue. Blue that is the place and no other place. Blue that is time and no other time. Blue about which they know everything there is to know, and before this blue no other blue.

Wendell Mayo was a native of Corpus Christi, Texas. He authored six collections of short stories, recently, What Is Said About Elephants with Unsolicited Press in 2020. His other collections are Survival House with SFASU Press; The Cucumber King of Kėdainiai, winner of the Subito Press Award for Innovative Fiction; Centaur of the North (Arte Público Press), winner of the Aztlán Prize; B. Horror and Other Stories (Livingston Press); and a novel-in-stories, In Lithuanian Wood (White Pine Press), which appeared in Lithuanian translation as Vilko Valanda [Engl: Hour of the Wolf] with Mintis Press in Vilnius. Over one-hundred of his short stories have appeared widely in magazines and anthologies, including Yale Review, Harvard Review, Manoa, Missouri Review, Boulevard, New Letters, Threepenny Review, Indiana Review, and Chicago Review. He received the National Endowment for the Arts Creative Writing Fellowship, a Fulbright to Lithuania (Vilnius University), two Individual Excellence Awards from the Ohio Arts Council, and a Master Fellowship from the Indiana Arts Commission. He taught fiction writing in the MFA/BFA programs at Bowling Green State University for over twenty years.